AWAKENED BY CANCER

A testimony of Faith and Hope

Susana Barrios

I

AWAKENED BY CANCER

A testimony of Faith and Hope

Title: **AWAKENED BY CANCER**
Subtitle: **A testimony of Faith and Hope**
Author: **Susana Barrios**
ISBN: 978-1-63895-041-7

Santillán Editorial
+1 (916) 308 - 3540
santillaneditorial@gmail.com

SANTILLAN

Acknowledgments

I want to express my deepest gratitude to my parents for doing the best they could to raise me and shower me with love. Additionally, I extend my heartfelt thanks to everyone who inspired me and believed in me, even when I struggled to believe in myself. My appreciation knows no bounds for those who never gave up on me, who recognized the goodness within me, who empathized with me, and who never judged me. To those who stood by me during my battle with cancer, providing nourishment, prayers, reaching out, and yes, even helping me tidy up my apartment – your kindness will forever reside in my heart. Special thanks go towards my husband and my children for their unwavering support during one of the most challenging periods of my life. To my family: Without you, I wouldn't be where I am today. Lastly, I want to express my gratitude to my angel, my grandma Lola. God knew how much I needed her, so He placed her in my life to represent Him. To this day, I deeply miss you!

Dedication

This book is dedicated to my kids, Austin and Hazel. You two are my motivation and my inspiration. You mean everything to me... I also want to dedicate this book to all my nieces and nephews. May you find in this pages the knowledge that it's possible to turn your pain into power. Never let your past define your present or your future.

"Life wanted to break me, but God brought me to this world to be an Overcomer."

– Susana–

About Me

My name is Susana Barrios, and I am happily married with two children of my own and three stepchildren. Faith is the cornerstone of my life; it's what propels me forward, and my faith means everything to me. I've endured various forms of abuse, both physical and emotional, but I've also triumphed over cancer. Through it all, I've transformed my pain into motivation to become a better person and to inspire others. Writing has always been a significant part of my life, serving as coping mechanisms and a way of expressing my emotions. My journey as a writer began in 5th grade when I penned my first book, a tale about a magic flower, which earned me an award. I have a deep love for magic and fairy tales; they enchant and inspire me. I strongly believe that everyone has a story to share, and there's someone out there waiting to hear it. For me, God is everything, and I hope that this book serves as an inspiration and source of hope for you.

Table of Contents

Introduction

In the pages that follow, you will journey alongside me, Susana Barrios, through my odyssey with a cancer diagnosis. But this is not merely a recounting of medical tests and treatments; it is a testimony to the transformative power of faith, resilience, and the unwavering presence of God in the face of life's greatest trials.

When cancer knocked on my door, it brought with it a new way of seeing life and an entirely different perspective. I discovered a strength I never knew I possessed: a strength rooted in my unwavering faith in God's divine purpose for my life. In the darkest moments of my illness, it was His light that guided me, His grace that sustained me, and His love that helped me push forward.

In these pages, you will witness the raw and unfiltered journey of a woman grappling with her mortality, seeking solace in the divine and ultimately emerging stronger, wiser, and more deeply connected to the divine presence that has guided her every step of the way. It is a story of redemption, of finding beauty in brokenness, and of discovering the true meaning of grace amidst suffering.

As you embark on this journey with me, I invite you to open your heart to the transformative power of faith, to embrace life's challenges with courage and resilience, and to trust in the unwavering love of a God who walks beside us through every valley and every mountain peak.

May this book serve as a beacon of hope for all who find themselves navigating the uncertain terrain of illness, adversity, and despair. May it remind you that, no matter how dark the night may seem, the dawn always breaks, and with it comes the promise of a new day filled with light, love, and the boundless grace of our heavenly Father.

XII

Chapter 1

Calling the Paramedics or Rushing Me to the Hospital

"What doesn't kill you, makes you stronger."

- Susana-

I remember being small and always getting sick. Every time I fell ill, I became the center of attention. I recall the trips to the hospital, with my dad rushing over from his parties—specifically, Pomona Valley Hospital—whenever he heard I was there. One of the reasons for my hospital visits was gastritis. They also diagnosed me with a form of asthma, and I seemed to catch the flu frequently. I cried often, sometimes so intensely that it seemed like I might faint, prompting calls to the ambulance. The paramedics even advised my mom to try to keep me from crying so much. It felt like there was always something wrong with me as I grew up. I suffered from frequent nosebleeds, waking up to find blood all over me. And then there were the parasites. It's not pleasant to recall, but it's the reality.

I remember going to the bathroom and seeing worms come out, having to call for my mom's help. I apologize for the graphic detail, but it's what happened.

Looking back, I realize that the only time I received attention was when I was sick, as if being healthy and strong was somehow less deserving of care. We often reserve our attention, love, and compassion for those going through hardships. We need to normalize visiting people when they're healthy, celebrating their lives while they're still here, instead of waiting until they're gone to celebrate them.

I was a fearful child and teenager. Loneliness frightened me, as did the prospect of moving out and living on my own. I was also rebellious, prone to talking back. If I couldn't grasp something, I couldn't obey it. I always strove to be true to myself, never one to pretend or wear a mask.

I always say, what you see is what you get. I've always felt like I was older and more mature for my age, or maybe life just forced me to grow up faster. I grew up to be constantly aware of my surroundings. I observed things keenly and always told myself I didn't want to become like that; I wanted a life that truly reflected who I am. I always stood up for my beliefs and never succumbed to peer pressure. I possessed a strength that surpassed such influences. If I wanted to do something, I did it; if not, then I didn't. Not everyone shares my perspective, and that's okay. This was just me, and I learned not to compare myself to others.

I felt as though God had chosen me from birth. I've always had faith in God, even from a young age; I remember praying for the first time when I was around eight years old, and I still recall the contents of that prayer. However, I also remember feeling like God never answered that prayer. As time passed, I came to realize that while we can pray for people to change, God won't force change upon them. This realization posed one of my biggest existential questions: why would God place me in the home I had, with parents who subjected me to so much suffering? It's something I may never comprehend or find an answer to. I don't believe we choose our parents; if you do, that's fine, but I don't share that belief. Why would I subject myself to such circumstances? Only God knows why certain things happen, and sometimes we must find peace in not having all the answers.

I've also learned not to judge others; everyone is doing the best they can with the resources they have, whether we perceive it or not. We need to extend grace to one another, especially considering that many of us grew up in homes where our emotional needs were often neglected. I've learned to embrace my past, live fully in the present, and accept the things I can no longer change. I only look back to glean lessons and to motivate myself. While I can't change my past, I can shape my present and my future, and that's the work I've been engaged in. Knowing that I am the architect of my own future brings me joy; we have the freedom to choose and to change. We can't change where we come from, but we have the power to change where we're headed.

Growing up for many years, I felt like a victim, as if life was targeting me and constantly throwing challenges my way. Everyone around me, including my family, knew about my struggles. It seemed that mistreatment was a recurring theme in my life, reinforcing my victim mentality. At one point, I even questioned if I was adopted. It was incomprehensible to me that parents could treat their child in such a way.

I vividly recall my grandmother on my father's side once confiding in me about my conception. She revealed that my parents didn't initially want me because my mother became pregnant unexpectedly, and adding to their disappointment, I was a girl. According to my grandmother, my father's displeasure during my mother's pregnancy led her to believe that I would inherit his traits. And indeed, I felt like I am a female version of him. Despite my longing for a relationship with my father, I never truly had one. Yet, there was a time when I idealized him, as many young girls do. I even envisioned marrying someone similar to him – hardworking and dedicated.

Understanding the circumstances of my conception and upbringing brought me a sense of peace and clarity. It allowed me to comprehend the roots of my struggles and the dynamics within my family. I believe that our experiences during pregnancy, even before birth, shape our perceptions and relationships. It's where the journey of life begins, where the fight for survival starts, and where our beliefs take root. Discovering that God had a purpose for me, as mentioned in the Bible, filled me with a sense of relief and significance.

Sometimes, we may consider ourselves accidents, but I believe that God's plan and choice give us purpose. Despite what our parents may think, God's selection and creation of us means a divine intention and a destined path.

I've always had faith in God, believing that my prayers would be answered. Despite facing challenges, I felt strong, capable of enduring whatever came my way. At one point, I accepted suffering as my fate, finding a strange peace in it.

My upbringing was marked by struggle and strife, shaping me into a person I hardly recognized. Constantly on the defensive, always ready for a verbal battle, and finding solace in alcohol, I took pride in my ability to drink. In my community, being a drinker was a badge of honor, reinforcing my identity. Yet, beneath these labels lay a deeper truth: we often wear masks that conceal our true selves, losing sight of who we really are.

I believe that each of us has a fundamental essence, defined by our unique traits and preferences. But as life unfolds, we lose sight of our inner light, consumed by fear and uncertainty. I've always felt different, seeing the world through a different lens and anticipating the consequences of my actions. Despite my independence, starting work at a young age, I found discomfort in relying on others for financial support. Despite the challenges, I found joy in giving, whether through shopping or helping my family. There's a profound satisfaction in giving to others, a sense of purpose that transcends personal struggles.

My grandma was my lifeline, my guardian angel, the rock that steadied me in turbulent times. Just knowing she was there brought me solace and reassurance. I'd reach out to her for prayer, and spending nights at her house felt like being in heaven, enveloped in a peace and joy I found nowhere else. She wasn't just a believer; she lived and breathed her faith. To me, she embodied true love, an earthly angel always ready to lend a hand. Her kindness knew no bounds, and her warmth extended to everyone she met.

Having such a wonderful grandma was a blessing beyond measure, an experience my own children never had the chance to share. I was fortunate to be loved and cherished by grandparents on both sides, and for that, I'm grateful.

This is my story, told through my lens, capturing the essence of how I lived and felt it. I've come to understand that broken individuals often perpetuate brokenness, a realization that took me years to come to terms with. Now, as a parent myself, I grapple with this truth, striving to protect my children from the pain I endured. Yet, I've learned that true healing begins within oneself; you cannot save others until you've saved yourself.

Broken parents raise broken kids; we are a mirror of who our parents are or were. Not until you're grown or until you're aware, you don't have to stay that way. You have a choice! But in order to have a choice, you need to stop being a victim!

Little did I know, my body and soul were broken, and my health was a way of crying for help. As kids, we don't know how to express ourselves; we don't know how to articulate what is wrong. Honestly, as adults, we still struggle with that.

This book is not focused on the abuses I received. Later

on in life, as I grew older, I came to understand that my illnesses were a manifestation of my suffering, a cry for help from my emotional pain. This realization dawned upon me as I grappled with various emotional and physical issues. When a child is crying or acting out, even as a teenager, it's crucial to understand that there's often a deeper problem behind those tears that may not be immediately visible.

Susana Barrios

Chapter 2

Grandma Lola

"We are here to be an inspiration."

- Susana-

I'll never forget how proud I used to feel, facing life's challenges head-on. I felt like I could handle anything, as if I had this inner strength that nothing could shake. It was almost like I embraced suffering, believing that the more I endured, the stronger I became. Suffering seemed woven into the fabric of my existence, just another part of daily life.

But when you experience so much pain, it's like you reach a point where you become numb. At least, that's how it happened for me. There were times when I cried myself to sleep, the weight of my struggles almost suffocating. It felt like suffering wasn't just a part of my life; it was my life.

That's not to say there weren't moments of happiness sprinkled in between. I'm sure there were, although I struggle to recall many of them. But when my grandma passed away, it felt like a piece of me was torn away. Life suddenly felt emptier, lonelier. I began to question my faith, grappling with feelings of abandonment. She was never sick, so her sudden death came as a shock. I remember the day vividly, the moment the phone call came and shattered my world. I can still see the sadness in her eyes the last time I saw her. She was my rock, my connection to God and peace. I would turn to her for prayers, finding solace in her presence, especially during those nights spent at her cozy little house.

For years, I lived in denial, unable to accept that she was gone. How could God take her away from me? How could He do that to me? My grandma was my refuge, especially when my mother's actions left me in tears. I would seek solace in her cottage, pouring out my heart to her. She would just shake her head and say, "Huh, your mom" Everyone knew how I was treated; it wasn't a secret to anyone. I often found myself seeking shelter at my uncle's house, unable to bear being home. That's why they called me "the streetwalker"

My house was the last place I wanted to be. Spending the night at my grandma's house was the best. Now I understand why God placed her in my life. He knew I would need her. She was our neighbor; I remember being small and going to her house on Sundays was routine. She was deeply involved with the church. I recall walking with her to church, back when people walked everywhere. My grandma loved helping people; her house was always bustling with visitors seeking remedies for various ailments — she healed general discomforts, and many others. Her little house was filled with plants; the front yard boasted all kinds of foliage for different remedies. Back then, home remedies were the norm, unlike now, where medication is the go-to solution. You can't mention an ailment without someone prescribing medication right away.

My grandma would pray her rosary every night; spending the night with her meant joining in the rosary prayers too. Praying the rosary took about thirty to forty minutes, though it felt like hours. It seemed dull at times, especially when we had to pray on our knees. My grandma was deeply devoted to God; I remember her always reading her bible, spending countless hours engrossed in its pages. During the nights I stayed over, I would walk past her room to the restroom and often find her there, reading her books late into the night. She also made regular donations to a church in Texas; every time she sent money, she would include a heartfelt note on the card. My grandma affectionately called me Tana.

That was my nickname, and she was the only one who called me Tana. My grandma had birds; I have this image of her in the front yard, cleaning her bird's cage. She adored her birds. My grandma used to regale us with stories, many from her time in Mexico. She had a remarkable testimony; someone had cast witchcraft upon her, and she fell terribly ill, nearly losing her sanity. They took her to a traditional healer, and she found liberation. After that, she came to the USA and dedicated her life to God.

There's so much to say about my grandma. Grandparents play an indispensable role in our lives and in the lives of our children. The way grandparents influence us, for better or worse, is inevitable. Not everyone has this experience; I wish my kids could have had it. I wish they could have stories to pass down to their kids, stories like mine or yours. That's why my grandma's passing meant so much to me. It changed my life forever. She was like a mother to me, a maternal figure in my life. Even after all these years, I still think about her, I still miss her, but I know she's my angel. She has been my angel, and I've experienced things that confirm she's in heaven, always watching over me wherever I am.

As I sit here, reminiscing about Grandma Lola, I find myself engulfed in a flood of memories, each one a testament to her enduring impact on my life. She was more than just a grandmother; she was a guiding light, illuminating the darkest corners of my soul with her love and wisdom.

In the days following her passing, grief consumed me like a relentless tide, pulling me deeper into its murky depths with each passing moment. The emptiness left in her absence was a void too vast to comprehend, a gaping wound in the fabric of my existence. I longed for her comforting presence, her reassuring voice, but all I found was silence—a deafening silence that echoed with the weight of her absence.

In the midst of my sorrow, I found solace in the memories we shared, in the laughter that once filled her cozy little house. I remembered the warmth of her embrace, the scent of her homemade remedies wafting through the air, and for a fleeting moment, it felt as though she was still with me, guiding me through the darkness with her gentle touch.

But as the days turned into weeks, and the weeks into months, the pain of her loss began to ebb, replaced by a bittersweet longing for what once was. I found myself seeking refuge in the familiar rituals of our time together— the nightly prayers, the stories she would tell, the simple joy of being in her presence. It was in those moments that I felt closest to her, as though she was reaching out from beyond the veil to reassure me that she was still with me, watching over me with the same love and care she had always shown.

And so, as I navigate the complexities of life without her by my side, I find comfort in the knowledge that her legacy lives on in the hearts of those she touched. She may no longer be physically present, but her spirit continues to guide me, a beacon of hope in a world often shrouded in darkness.

In the end, Grandma Lola's passing was not just a loss; it was a testament to the enduring power of love—a love that transcends even the boundaries of death itself. And though I may never fully understand why she was taken from me, I take comfort in knowing that she is at peace, her spirit free to soar among the stars, forever watching over me with the same love and devotion she showed in life.

Susana Barrios

Chapter 3

My Emotions Don't Count

"It's possible to turn your pain into power."

- Susana-

I was codependent, though I didn't realize it then. Always worried about everyone else's needs, never mine. Always wrapped up in helping my parents, I gave them everything, leaving nothing for myself. It's not wrong to support your parents, but it has to be balanced. When your codependent, you're giving from an empty place. I started paying rent the moment I got a job. I remember my parents constantly fighting, it seemed like it never stopped. Dad's threats to leave were a constant backdrop in our lives. His drinking was a problem, and he always had high blood pressure. Mom, well, she was neurotic. She raised us to compete, not to unite. When you're young, you don't realize your parents are flawed; you just love them, no matter what. They're your first experience of love, the ones who mold you. How they love you shapes how you understand love.

Most of the attention was on Dad because of his health issues. We walked on eggshells, fearing he'd have a heart attack. And if something we did made his heart race, it was our fault. I didn't know then that alcohol made it worse. But that's the thing in dysfunctional families or where there's alcoholism, all the attention goes to the one with the problem. Alcoholism ran in Dad's family, and high blood pressure ran in Grandma's family.

I was so caught up in my codependency that I thought I'd never get married because I wanted to take care of Dad forever. Who thinks like that? It's all about balance. I did help them, always, in every way I could. Looking back, I wish I'd left sooner. I didn't realize there was another life out there where I could be happy, where my feelings mattered, where I deserved the best.

When you are small, the worst is not just being physically abused, the worst for me was not being able to defend myself and repressing all those angry feelings of how it felt to be hit and not being able to do anything about it, but built up hate. I hated my mom for that and throughout the years I just built up more and more anger towards her. I hated my dad for never defending me and because he was always working and drinking. I built so much anger through my life. My mom was physically abusive until I was 17. The last time she hit me I remember being like 17 and she hit me with a broom. The image that I have from my mom is the image of a mom hitting a child. I am not saying she wasn't nice at times or she didn't hug me but I don't have a memory like that.

I was not living; I was always surviving. Partying, drinking was my escape, that part of my life I always remember liking. Where I was able to be myself. Doing things that seemed fun at the moment and that made me happy! I never liked to be home, it was always hard for me, I rather be in the street than being at my house. I was always a free spirited person, or someone who had trouble following rules per se. Some house rules did not make sense to me, especially after supporting myself and paying my rent. But you already know, in Mexican families you need to follow rules as long as you live with your parents no matter how old you are.

In the midst of everything I always wanted to get married. Have a wedding with my white dress. That was a dream that i always had, in the midst of everything I guess i still believed in marriage. How? God had a plan for me. When I found out my dad had cheated on my mom, I stopped believing in marriage for a little bit. In the midst of it all, I still had my dad on a pedestal, I had to bring him down. I had to acknowledge that he was not perfect, that he was human and that we all make mistakes, all kinds of mistakes. For a bit I was disappointed, my dad always seemed the kind of person to be honest but what can I expect of someone that gets married drunk? When my mom told us the story that my dad was drunk the day they got married, I thought it was funny, I feel things that start not good will most likely not be good in the future. Because they were not honest with each other and that became their lifestyle and that's how they raised their four daughters. I think the foundation is key for long lasting good relationships. What you do in the process will determine how things unfold.

As time passes and we got older, we begin to realize that our parents are just as broken, if not more so, than we are. They did the best they could with what they had at the time to raise us. They simply didn't know any better. When we delve into their stories, we start to understand the reasons behind their actions. However, understanding their story doesn't excuse their behavior, actions, or abuses. If it was abuse, let's call it what it is. If it was toxic, let's recognize it as such. Healing requires us to confront things for what they truly are.

Family is laden with beliefs and traditions. Each family holds its own set of beliefs, like the notion that family always comes first. We're taught to honor our parents, regardless of their actions towards us, to love and respect them unconditionally. This notion is deeply flawed, trapping many of us in abusive situations because we fear disappointing or hurting our parents. We attend family gatherings where we're expected to greet with kisses, even those relatives we dislike or who've mistreated us, to avoid being labeled as disrespectful. We're groomed to please everyone around us, to prioritize their happiness over our own, to suppress our feelings, and to deny ourselves the right to express them. Speaking out about our thoughts or emotions only creates trouble.

We learn the saying, "quiet you look prettier," because speaking up for ourselves is seen as problematic. From a young age, I possessed a strong character, observing the lives of those around me and recognizing that their way of living wasn't what I desired or what I was willing to tolerate.

My outspoken nature made me the black sheep, as I refused to stay silent about injustices I witnessed. Yet, despite my strength, I still lost myself along the way. Without a solid foundation, lacking guidance and protection, I sought solace in places and activities that offered temporary relief from the void within me.

Moreover, we're instilled with the belief that blood relations take precedence, compelling us to prioritize others over ourselves for fear of betraying the family.

When you show the courage to speak up and express your desire not to follow in their footsteps, prepare yourself, because they'll quickly cast you as the villain, loading you with guilt for simply yearning to carve out your own path and craft a life distinct from theirs. It strikes me deeply that many of our parents, perhaps unknowingly, sought to live vicariously through us, endeavoring to achieve their own unfulfilled dreams and aspirations through our endeavors.

It's a common pitfall—one too many of us fall into—we strive to shield our children from repeating our own missteps or enduring worse fates, thus we impose upon them the very pursuits we failed to realize ourselves. Yet, the tragedy lies in our failure to recognize or acknowledge this dynamic most of the time. As the sands of time continue to trickle away, we gradually come to understand that each child born into this world arrives with their own unique mission and purpose in life, one that must be discovered and navigated independently, even if it means confronting their own trials and tribulations.

Life, in its complexity, often proves to be a journey riddled with hardships, trials that not only shape us but often compel us to our knees—yet, paradoxically, they frequently unveil themselves as blessings in disguise, fostering growth and resilience within us. From the earliest days of childhood, we're conditioned to distrust our own instincts, with our parents assuming the role of arbiters over our lives—dictating curfews, selecting our friends, prescribing our career paths, even determining our attire and hairstyle.

Our autonomy is systematically stripped away, leaving us bereft of the ability to make our own choices; instead, every decision is made on our behalf. Consequently, we evolve into fearful, hesitant adults, tethered to our parents by invisible threads, unsure of how to venture forth into the world on our own. I, too, lingered within the confines of my parent's home for what felt like an eternity, oblivious to the toxicity of my surroundings until the passage of time afforded me a clearer perspective. Why? Because familiarity breeds comfort, and the known, however detrimental, becomes our sole reality—even if it proves to be our undoing.

This was my truth, my reality—but perhaps for someone else, it's the norm. Yet, for me, it wasn't. Growing up amidst the shadow of alcoholism, surrounded by its pervasive influence throughout my entire existence, instilled within me a fervent desire to shield my own children and future husband from such a grim fate. Reflecting on my past, I now recognize the eerie similarities between my own marriage and the dynamics of my parents' relationship—or what passed for one, at least. I vividly recall yearning to flee the suffocating confines of home, desperately seeking sanctuary in a place of safety and solace, only to find myself ensnared in familiar or even more treacherous circumstances.

When you're young and desperate, clarity often eludes you; any form of attention, even negative, feels better than none at all. I vividly recall the moment my father discovered I had spent the night with him—he promptly insisted I move in with him because, in his eyes, I was no longer pure. Interestingly, my sisters, at the tender age of 15, had already fled our home.

My father had pinned all his hopes and dreams on me, perhaps because my three sisters hadn't pursued higher education, and he clung to the hope that I would be the exception. Yet, instead of altering his behavior to ensure I wouldn't leave, he treated me even worse. I've come to believe that individuals grappling with alcoholism are often blind to the consequences of their actions; perpetually numbed, they fail to perceive reality for what it truly is, retreating into avoidance as a coping mechanism.

I can still vividly recall my father cracking open a beer every single day, and then some more on weekends. It's that ingrained belief that a beer soothes exhaustion or aids in restful sleep—such notions persist, even today. In my view, excessive drinking is a sign of discontentment with one's life, a perpetual attempt to escape from reality. In my father's case, it is not difficult to understand why he sought solace in alcohol. I have indelible memories of the parties and the inevitable fights that followed. My uncles, fueled by alcohol, would invariably descend into brawls, harboring resentment toward each other that, I suspect, still lingers to this day.

It all stems from how they were raised. We weren't brought up to foster harmony and cooperation; instead, we were thrust into a world where conflict and competition were the norm. I can still recall the absurdity of being forced into physical fights by my parents—what kind of upbringing condones such behavior? My parents were quick to denounce certain cousins as "crazy" and forbade us from associating with them, yet ironically, they labeled us with the same derogatory terms, dismissing our potential and belittling our aspirations.

Susana Barrios

Chapter 4

Beliefs or traditions

"Let pain be your motivation."

- Susana-

I recall a particular instance when a visitor came to our home—a professional, if memory serves me right. I can't quite recall who they were or why they were there; all I remember is the conversation that ensued. This individual spoke about potential career opportunities, suggesting avenues for us to pursue, yet I distinctly remember my father dismissing the notion, asserting that we weren't worthy of such pursuits. Looking back, I can't help but feel as though those words cast upon us a dark shadow, a curse of sorts.

Words possess a remarkable power; they cling to us, shaping our perceptions of ourselves, and with time, we internalize them, gradually becoming the very embodiment of those words. It's only now, with the benefit of hindsight, that I realize the profound impact words can have. People have the ability to bless or curse others with their words, and while we possess the power to resist their influence, as children, we're often oblivious to this fact. It's particularly devastating when these words come from those we hold dear, especially close family members, and even more so when they emanate from our own parents.

Throughout my upbringing, I carried with me a litany of labels—always the "ugly" one, the "lazy" one, the one with "ugly teeth" and an "ugly body." My eldest sister, my father's favorite, basked in his favor, embodying his ideal of perfection with her pleasing physique. Ana, the youngest, was the family's darling, her delicate features earning her the nickname "The Barbie." Then there was the other sister, hailed as the diligent one, the expert cleaner, particularly adept at tackling the refrigerator. I distinctly remember being chastised for my cleaning efforts, criticized for purportedly making more of a mess than before. I was told I couldn't wash dishes properly, and that my lack of domestic skills would condemn me to a life devoid of marriage or culinary prowess.

Amidst these disparaging remarks, there was one beacon of encouragement—my uncle. He consistently championed my academic pursuits, urging me to excel in school. I'll never forget the pride he displayed at my graduation, hosting a celebratory party in my honor and gifting me a graduation ring as a token of his belief in my potential. It's as though god conspired to place these supportive figures in my life when I needed them most. Even today, I'm surrounded by individuals who continue to propel me toward success, steadfast in their belief in my abilities, even during times when I doubted myself. Despite the barrage of negativity, there was one aspect of my identity that remained unscathed—my affinity for academia. I took solace in my intellect, feeling a sense of confidence and assurance that set me apart from my siblings.

From as far back as I can remember, I've always been the social butterfly of the family—the one with a plethora of friends, spreading warmth and cheer wherever I went. Unlike my siblings, I relished in the company of others, eagerly bringing friends home to mingle with the family. Looking back, I can't help but wonder why my mother was so adamant about prohibiting us from having friends over— what was she trying to shield us from? It's curious, now that I think about it, how my mother herself never seemed to have any friends of her own; I can't recall a single instance of visitors gracing our doorstep.

It's almost as if I was destined to break the cycle, to shatter the chains of isolation and estrangement that bound us together as a family. Perhaps that's why I was viewed as a threat—a daughter poised to defy convention, unafraid to sever ties and forge her own path, unyielding in her refusal to tolerate abuse, disrespect, or manipulation. Sadly, it took a battle with cancer to awaken me to the realization that I needed to stand up for myself and my children—to break free from the suffocating grip of manipulation and reclaim my autonomy. Until then, I had lived a life devoid of identity, devoid of purpose, adrift in a sea of uncertainty.

Amidst the turmoil, there were moments of triumph that I cherish to this day—milestones that served as beacons of hope amidst the darkness. I began earning money at the tender age of 14, carving out a semblance of financial independence for myself. By 16, I had purchased my own car, a testament to my determination and resourcefulness. And at 18, I proudly bought my first car from a dealership— an achievement that filled me with an unparalleled sense of pride and accomplishment.

I was always diligent about saving money, instilled with a sense of fiscal responsibility from a young age. I set my sights on my goals with unwavering determination, relentlessly pursuing success in the face of adversity. It's not typical for a child or teenager to shoulder such burdens, but not all of us had the luxury of parental support. I witnessed my father toil endlessly, working multiple jobs just to make ends meet, and I resolved early on to shoulder my own burdens, reluctant to rely on others for financial assistance.

Since I was a child, I've always had a giving nature. I used to give my sisters gifts to encourage them in school. On Father's and Mother's Day, I'd ask my dad for money to buy them something special, even if it was just $20. We didn't have a car growing up, so we had to walk to the laundromat, which I dreaded. Looking back, I wish I could remember more of my childhood. Writing this book is helping bring back some memories.

I've made peace with revisiting my past. I've healed a lot with God's help, and it's empowering to see how far I've come. I appreciate what my parents did for us. I remember my dad always working hard to provide for us, and my mom made sure we looked nice. She loved matching our clothes and doing our hair with little accessories. Laundry was always done by hand, and we often had to wear the same clothes every other day to avoid washing too often. I also remember one of my chores was fixing our shoes, which were stored in a drawer in the bathroom. Our living situation was modest; we lived in a studio apartment with one medium-sized bedroom, which doubled as my mom's room and the living area, furnished only with a couch.

The ambiance of our home, with its snug kitchen and slightly larger room compared to the restroom, felt like a hub connecting various passages of our humble abode. Imagine three doors, delineating distinct realms: one leading to the restroom, another to the kitchen, and the third to the outside world. Despite its modest size, I recall my mother's unwavering commitment to cleanliness. Our dwelling might not have been the grandest, but she infused it with a constant aura of tidiness and orderliness.

To traverse from the kitchen to my mother's room, one merely had to draw aside the curtains, for there was no solid partition. Ah, the ubiquitous curtains-as-walls phenomenon—a quintessential feature of many a Mexican household, and ours was no exception! It's a bit of cultural flair that always brings a smile.

Our dwelling, weathered by time, bore the scars of its age. When rain fell, our room became a sieve, droplets trickling through the roof like tears of an old soul. And when the winds picked up, it felt as though our little house might take flight, propelled by the sheer force of nature. I'll never forget the night when a window shattered, the sudden cacophony shattering the silence of slumber. It sent shivers down our spines, a moment of fear etched into our memories.

Just a stone's throw away resided my grandmother, in her quaint, diminutive dwelling adorned with an array of verdant foliage. Those plants weren't just decor—they were her apothecary, her arsenal against ailments. If ever one felt unwell, Grandma would prescribe a "small plant," her remedy for all manner of maladies. She was a beacon of care and compassion, a figure woven into the fabric of our community. Her home was a sanctuary, but her heart was the true refuge.

I fondly recall our walks to church, hand in hand, her faith unwavering and her devotion palpable. And oh, the church plays—Grandma, adorned in her costume, gracing the stage with a celestial presence. She was our family's guiding light; an earthly angel whose love knew no bounds. How I long for my children to have known her embrace, to bask in the warmth of her love.

Yet, amidst the fond memories, there lingers a shadow—a whisper of familial discord. My mother speaks of her own parents with a hint of sadness, of a love withheld or perhaps misdirected. It's a tale as old as time, the complexities of family dynamics playing out in subtle gestures and quiet resentments. Some aunts, I recall, were less than kind to my mother, their treatment a stark contrast to the warmth Grandma exuded. But even in the face of adversity, I stood by my mother's side, a stalwart defender against the cruelties of kinship.

Such is the tapestry of our lives, woven with threads of love and longing, of joy and sorrow. And amidst it all, Grandma's spirit lingers—a guiding star in the constellation of memory, illuminating the path forward with her boundless love.

To this day, my mother remains a complex figure, not easily understood or getting along with. Yet, as time has passed, I've come to realize that her life journey has been fraught with hardships, wounds left unhealed, and burdens carried without respite. It's a weight that can consume one's spirit, leaving behind a residue of sickness and bitterness. The path to healing, I've discovered, is no easy road; in fact, it may be one of the most arduous journeys one can undertake. For me, it's an ongoing process, a lifelong commitment to self-restoration.

But despite the challenges, I've come to embrace this journey with a sense of acceptance and even gratitude. Each step forward, no matter how small, fills me with a profound sense of joy and understanding. Yet, just when I think I've reached a place of peace, another hurdle presents itself, another layer to peel back. Such is the nature of life's complexities, but I wouldn't trade it for anything. Through awareness, I've found solace, and through understanding, I've learned to extend grace to myself.

It's easy to be harsh on oneself, to forget the struggles we've endured and the resilience it took to survive. I look back on my childhood, and much of it remains a blur, overshadowed by dissociation, —a coping mechanism to shield myself from a reality I couldn't bear to face or feel. Amidst the haze, though, there are moments of clarity, memories illuminated by the warmth of my grandmother's presence. In her home, I found refuge, a sanctuary of happiness and peace.

Reflecting on those early years, I'm struck by the constant presence of men in our household. Where did they sleep, I wonder now, with a hint of bemusement. It's a curious realization, growing up surrounded by male figures, with little privacy or sense of security. It was a common occurrence in Hispanic households, I believe, though I'm hopeful that times have changed. Such circumstances, I've come to understand, can create fertile ground for abuse—a cycle of victimization perpetuated through generations.

Yet, with age comes wisdom, and I've learned to see abusers not just as perpetrators but as victims themselves, caught in the tangled web of their own traumas. It's a realization that doesn't excuse their actions but offers a glimpse of empathy, a flicker of understanding. Forgiveness, if chosen, doesn't necessitate reconciliation; it's a choice made for one's own peace of mind, a reclaiming of power over one's own narrative.

I believe abuse is like a curse; often, it affects more than just one person in a family. It's like a cycle that keeps repeating until someone decides to break it. I know for sure that I've been that person—the one who decided to stop hiding family secrets, to face reality head-on. It's a liberating feeling, knowing that you weren't the problem, that as a child, you were a victim and it wasn't your fault.

As kids, we tend to blame ourselves for things that aren't our fault. Psychology tells us that children often blame themselves when bad things happen, thinking they must have done something wrong. This can mess with your head, making you a people-pleaser and making you feel like you're always at fault. It takes a lot of self-awareness to recognize this pattern and break free from it.

Healing means having a lot of conversations with yourself, believe it or not. You catch yourself repeating old behaviors, and you have to talk yourself out of them, bringing yourself back to the present moment. You have to remind yourself that you're not defined by your past, and sometimes, it's just your ego—the person you became to protect yourself—that's getting in the way.

We need to learn to leave the past behind, focus on the present, and embrace what's happening right now. That's how we create new opportunities, new adventures, and break free from old cycles.

Susana Barrios

Chapter 5

Awakening

"Mindset is everything."

- Susana-

This book is all about awakening, awakening that wonderful, beautiful, and smart person we have inside each of us. It's about refusing to let our past define our present or future. It's about not allowing time to slip away while we remain trapped in the past, unable to fully embrace the present. We all have a story to tell, a story that holds power, a story that could unlock someone else's door. Perhaps someone out there is waiting for us to share our story so they can find connection and understanding. They need to see that they're not alone, that others have faced similar struggles. It's not enough to dismiss their experiences by saying, "It happens to everyone" or "It's common." Doing so invalidates their feelings and journey. What matters is that is happening to them, and that's significant.

We've grown accustomed to normalizing so many experiences that we've become desensitized and lost touch with empathy. We hardly react when others are hurting. It's like we've forgotten the importance of kindness and the fact that everyone is fighting battles we know nothing about. Simple gestures—a smile, a moment of our time—can brighten someone's day. When we extend ourselves to others, whether through material things or our time, we're also enriching our own lives. It's a universal law: what we give to others, we receive in return.

In reality, we all need each other. We weren't meant to navigate life alone or to endure loneliness. Having good people in our lives is a blessing. It's having someone to trust in, someone who listens without judgment, someone who stands by us when no one else does. There will be moments in life when we find ourselves alone, and while these moments may force us to rely solely on ourselves, they also strengthen us, reinforcing the belief that we have everything we need within us.

If we take the time to listen to our inner voice, whatever name we give it—I call it God, the Holy Spirit—we'll find that divine presence within us. I believe God is with me, residing within me, and whenever I call upon Him, He provides the answers and guidance I seek. But it requires trust and faith. We don't listen to our intuition, our inner wisdom, as much as we should.

Even when we do listen to it, we don't trust it. We convince ourselves it's not real, that we're just imagining things or that it's something we can't rely on. That's when we start seeking external validation or turning to others for answers. It's not necessarily wrong to seek help, but sometimes the people we lean on are no better off than we are, or they may not have our best interests at heart. As I mentioned before, from a young age, I've had faith in God. Since childhood, I've felt that God always granted my requests. How did I arrive at this point? How did I navigate through life's challenges? It's because of Him, that inner voice, that strength that comes solely from Him. We're raised not to trust ourselves.

Writing this book has been an incredible journey; it's something I've always dreamed of doing. I would often start but never finish, and now I understand why. When things are meant to unfold and the timing is right, inspiration strikes, doors open, and everything flows effortlessly, without coercion. It's beautiful when you allow yourself to be guided and let things fall into place naturally, in their own time. I've never felt this inspired or motivated before. It makes me believe that now is the time, that there's someone out there in the world seeking healing, and I hope this book can assist many women, and even men, on their journeys. We all face challenges, struggles, and hardships, but not everyone confronts a serious illness like cancer and shares their experiences openly. The fear of vulnerability is understandable. It's not easy to open up about your past and the experiences that have shaped you. But eventually, you reach a point where you can embrace vulnerability, where you can speak your truth without shame or concern about others' reactions. That's true freedom.

Real freedom is embracing yourself fully, being unapologetically you, and walking your path without worrying about others' opinions. It's the ability to confidently say yes when you need to and no when it's necessary. Making decisions based on what's best for you without doubting yourself is a significant milestone in your healing journey. It's particularly challenging to do so when you've been codependent. Recognizing my own codependency and realizing I'd been that way for so long was incredibly difficult. It was tough to acknowledge that I'd been doing things for others without anyone asking me to. Breaking free from that pattern was a monumental task for me.

I've played the role of everyone's savior my entire life. I was the decision-maker, the problem-solver, the one who even chose the names for kids, not even my own kids. I lived to please and rescue everyone, forgetting about myself in the process, always putting myself last. I constantly prioritized everyone else's needs and feelings above my own, choosing people who didn't choose me back. I was helping the same people who were causing me pain and breaking me down. Why? Because I didn't have a life or identity of my own. I existed outside of myself, as if my physical body resided on Earth while my mind and spirit were elsewhere.

I never truly experienced connection, affection, or love like that, so I didn't realize I was missing it until I learned to love and accept myself and put myself first. You can't miss what you've never known or had. You get used to whatever you have, unaware that there might be something different and better beyond your current existence. I didn't know how to live a life full of joy, to play like a child, because it felt like my childhood was stolen from me. Even if I tried to be carefree like a child, I didn't know how. It was difficult. I remember attending a church retreat once where we were asked to revisit our childhood. They encouraged us to pretend to be children again, to play with toys and dolls. When it was time to play, I was lost. I didn't know how to act like a child. I remember having Barbie dolls, a pink Barbie Corvette, and a little Barbie closet. I liked playing with Barbies.

Children are innocent, playful, fearless. I feel like I lost that innocence at a young age. I didn't experience it, so it was hard to change my serious demeanor and learn to be playful, to have fun, and to enjoy the small things in life. Most importantly, I struggled to learn to relax. I was always on high alert, hyper-vigilant. When I started practicing meditation, it was incredibly challenging. My mind raced with thoughts at lightning speed. To relax is to be present in the moment. Now, I cherish my quiet moments, the times when it's just me, with my thoughts and feelings.

You can't relax or find peace if you're always dwelling on the past or worrying about the future. I'm not suggesting that you'll lead a stress-free life—frankly, I don't think that's feasible. What I do mean is giving yourself moments throughout the day to just be still, to relax, to breathe. Breathing is incredibly important, yet it's something we often overlook. Our lives are so fast-paced; we're constantly on autopilot. We forget to pause and truly experience the gift of being alive, of breathing, of being grateful for what we have. Waking up every day is a blessing, one that we sometimes take for granted. At least, I know I did, until cancer came and reminded me of everything I had been blessed with by God—the life I had been given. It came to shake me awake, to offer me a second chance.

Cancer taught me the importance of living one day at a time. Tomorrow isn't guaranteed, so worrying about it means missing out on today. Today will never come again; the opportunities I have, the moment I open my eyes won't return. We're so used to worrying about the future that it's difficult to relax. If we're not worrying, it feels like something's missing. Our bodies have become accustomed to stress for so long that if we're not stressed, we don't feel quite right; it's almost as if we're missing a familiar sensation. It's like the saying goes: if you're always complaining, you're signaling to life that you need more reasons to complain each day. If you're always stressed, you're telling life that you need problems to keep you stressed. It's manifestation—our thoughts become feelings, which later materialize into realities.

I remember when I first discovered the power of my words and thoughts; I became aware of it at just eleven years old. We had this thing in our hands called pimples; it was like an infection, contagious. I recall my sisters getting them first, and the older ones being more fearful and affected by them. It was like some kind of fungus, nasty-looking.

When I witnessed my sisters getting those pimples, I told myself, "I'm not going to get them like that." And sure enough, I didn't. It's something that has stuck with me because, even as a child, I knew that thoughts have power. I'm not sure how I knew, but I just did. We have the ability to use our thoughts and words to create— we're constantly creating, whether we're aware of it or not. What we do, feel, and think now will shape what's to come. Of course, it's easier said than done. To control our thoughts and words, we have to be fully present in the moment, which is something we often struggle with. When I catch myself slipping into negativity, I make a conscious effort to snap out of it. I believe that a lot of illnesses are from this—feeling something, diagnosing ourselves, and inadvertently bringing it into reality. It's funny because even as I write this, I catch myself saying, "I have this and that!"

I've heard that cancer is linked to unforgiveness, stress, holding grudges, and so on. But honestly, only God knows. The purpose of this book is to share how cancer changed my life—my life before cancer versus my life after cancer. I can't explain the transformation without delving into the backstory—where I come from, how I got to where I am, and the belief that our bodies often reveal what we don't articulate with words. Sicknesses come to help us heal our souls, our spiritual selves. Everyone who has endured a severe illness will recount their experiences differently, through their own lens, based on their feelings and perceptions. There will be those who agree or disagree, but I believe it's more important to accept and respect each other's unique perspectives and stories. I feel that, ultimately, we're all connected in some way.

Now is the time for me to share, to open up about my journey, to have a dialogue with you—yes, you, the one reading this book. This isn't just about someone who was physically ill; it's about someone who was mentally and emotionally unwell. It's about finding light in the midst of darkness, about discovering blessings in disguise. I never imagined that cancer would give me my life back, that it would change my life forever—for the better. Despite this positive outcome for me, it wasn't an easy journey. I wouldn't wish it to anyone. It's like teetering on the edge of death, not knowing whether you'll make it through or not.

I remember being young, sitting on the couch, sipping juice, and thinking, "One day, I'm going to get sick." I don't recall if I was specifically thinking about cancer. I'm not even sure if it was a real memory or just a dream— haha! When you're in a deeply negative place in life, you start expecting the worst to happen; it becomes almost a way of life, so the bad news doesn't surprise you anymore. It's incredibly challenging to envision positive things for your future or to believe that life could possibly wish the best for you, or that you deserve good things.

I recall looking around me and, despite yearning for a different life, I couldn't see how that was ever going to happen. I didn't have a frame of reference for what a good or better life might look like. I always looked up to Aunt Chona; she seemed to have the life I wanted. She was intelligent, she married her soulmate, and she had a beautiful wedding in a white dress. Though she could be a bit stern, she had the things I desired because she appeared happy and had achieved her goals. Unlike the tumultuous marriages I witnessed around me, hers stood out as peaceful, without fights or alcohol. I remember spending nights at her house, observing how well she and Uncle Chato got along—it seemed idyllic. Her home felt warm and welcoming, unlike anywhere else I'd been. She had always been brilliant, and I always admired her determination. Many years later, I confided in her about my feelings, and she shared that she felt the same way about me all along. They say that when you see something admirable in someone, it's because you possess it too.

Despite our similarities, Aunt Chona and I often clashed. She's one of many people who taught me not to trust; I once shared a secret with her, and she betrayed my trust by telling my parents, causing me to never fully trust her again. In the kind of environment, I was raised in, trust was a rare commodity; in fact, it was something I struggled to extend to anyone. When you're brought up in an atmosphere like mine, you learn not to trust because it feels like nobody can be relied upon and that everyone is out to hurt you. So, unsurprisingly, you end up attracting exactly that. Finding someone you can trust, someone who makes you feel safe, is invaluable — it's like finding a precious gem. I am truly blessed to have such people in my life, more than one friend whom I can trust and with whom I can be myself. As you start to heal, you begin to trust again; you start to believe that there are people with good intentions, that not everyone is out to hurt you.

We grow up with fear, and over time, as we embark on our healing journey, that fear begins to dissipate. It never truly disappears, but we learn to control it, to conquer it instead of letting it overpower us. The words spoken to us during our formative years, the things we witness, and how we're treated shape us into someone we're not. This affects our adult lifestyle, influencing the choices we make and the partners we choose in life. I vividly recall my days working in a seafood restaurant when a customer told me that I'd never succeed in school, in college to be precise, because of my upbringing. Those words stuck with me indefinitely; even today, I remember them vividly. I think that's why I was so insistent on my kids excelling in education—I wanted them to believe that they could achieve anything they set their minds to, that they could attend college, graduate, and earn a degree. I always tell them that going to school and obtaining a degree is a gift to ourselves. Even if they don't immediately use it, it's something that will remain on their resume forever, something that nobody can take away from them.

Yesterday, while watching a movie on Hulu about Frito Lay, I look back to a time when I reconnected with my high school best friend. By then, I already had children, while she worked or still works for Frito Lay. As she spoke about her life and career, her travels and accomplishments, I couldn't help but feel insignificant.

She seemed to have it all—a fulfilling life, a loving husband, while I was struggling to survive in the world.

It's all a mental barrier—all the obstacles we face are rooted within us, stemming from the words, beliefs, and experiences that don't truly belong to us. These are things that were said or done to us during our childhood or early adulthood, but we've internalized them as part of our identity. I'm amazed at how I managed to maintain a positive attitude and a smile throughout my life. I won't deny it; I've never been always kind. Controlling my emotions, especially when provoked, has always been a challenge for me. It's difficult for me to remain silent and keep my thoughts to myself, particularly when faced with injustice. We live in a world where people can be cruel and hurtful. Yes, those who hurt others are often hurting themselves, but that doesn't excuse or justify their actions. Even today, I struggle to hold my tongue, especially when something feels unjust. There are certain triggers that will always affect me. You can heal, but there are deep scars that never truly fade. Learning to live with them is part of the journey — understanding what triggers you, what brings you sadness or joy.

I've spent the majority of my life striving to please others, constantly doing things for them, aiming to make them happy. I was always the host, the one to organize everything, to cater to everyone's needs. I recall attending family gatherings during the holidays because it was expected of me, because we were family, because I had to go. But one day, it dawned on me—I was seeking approval and acceptance. I would attend these gatherings, but I never truly enjoyed myself. Instead, I often felt discontent. There were always remarks and actions that left me feeling unsettled. Yet, they were family; after all, family always comes first. Deep down, my inner child still yearned for that sense of family, that love, that acceptance, and validation.

Breaking cycles takes immense effort. It requires the courage to say no, to push back against expectations, especially when you start creating your own family and establish your own traditions. It was during my time at my mom's house that I started to become more aware of this dynamic.

Susana Barrios

Chapter 6

Trusting in God's Purpose

"God is an expert in turning a mess into a Blessing."

- Susana-

I found myself in my thirties, still dwelling under my parents' roof, gripped by fear at the mere thought of venturing out on my own. The weight of responsibilities, particularly those concerning my children, bore down on me, suffocating any courage I might have summoned. Remaining nestled in my parents' abode seemed the safest choice; after all, my mother's assistance in caring for my children was invaluable, though I always made sure to contribute financially.

As I entered my late twenties, a restlessness consumed me, driving me into the arms of nightlife and the solace of alcohol. Many of us seek refuge in various distractions, oblivious to the chasm growing within us. Why? Because these distractions become our norm, blinding us to their detrimental effects. For me, revelry, alcohol, and stress were constants, ingrained in my existence without question. I immersed myself in partying while my children slept, naively believing they remained unaware, only to discover later that they felt my absence, with my daughter's tears and my son's consoling presence revealing the truth.

In times of personal anguish, the welfare of others often eludes us, and despite my efforts, I failed to shield my children from the consequences of my choices. My focus shifted to maintaining a facade of busyness and numbing the harsh realities of my life. Meanwhile, my children endured confinement to a single room for years, deprived of basic comforts and sustenance. I refrain from delving into the harrowing details here; they do not belong in these pages.

My social circle consisted largely of companions who sought me out solely for the allure of revelry. Yet, I've come to understand that true friends seek your well-being above all else. Our living conditions were dire, housed in an uninsulated garage where cold penetrated our bones in winter, and sweltering heat stifled us in summer. Gratitude fills me for my parents' hospitality, though they were unaware of the toll it took. Friends visited, yet remained silent witnesses to our plight, until one courageous soul, visiting during the summer heatwave, confronted the stark reality of our living conditions. "How can you endure this?" she exclaimed, igniting a spark of introspection within me.

It was then that I began to question the path I was on; to recognize the harm I was inflicting upon my children. Anxiety gnawed at me as the battle between my desires for change and the paralyzing grip of fear waged within.

I began to feel incredibly overwhelmed, lost in a maze of confusion. The fear stemming from the manipulation I endured at the hands of my mother felt like being trapped in a suffocating mental prison. Whenever I entertained thoughts of breaking free, she would unleash threats and guilt upon me, chaining me to her side for years on end. I longed for assistance, yet the thought of leaving and something happening to them burdened me with guilt. How could I have prioritized them over my own children for so long? The answer lay in my deep-seated need for them, ingrained by years of familial obligation and a profound fear of causing them suffering or abandonment.

This fear, a constant feeling since childhood, haunted me relentlessly. Then, one cloudy day, my children's innocent musings about Jesus's sadness when it rained sparked a curiosity about God. Raised without religious teachings, I scrambled to placate their inquiries with movies about God, desperate to avoid uncomfortable questions I couldn't answer.

Around January 27, 2008, a profound confusion descended upon me like a dense fog. I stood in front of the mirror, staring at my reflection yet feeling detached, as though observing myself from afar with blurred vision. Each passing day deepened my disorientation, pushing me perilously close to the brink of insanity. With my mother away in Mexico that week, I feared her return, dreading the possibility of her noticing my unraveling mind.

I retreated into my room upon returning from work, consumed by the chaos brewing within me. Strangely, I cannot recall the whereabouts of my children during those tumultuous moments, lost in the whirlwind of my own unraveling thoughts. I reached out to my sisters, pleading for solitude as I grappled with an inexplicable turmoil. Upon hearing of my distress, my aunt offered a spiritual explanation, insisting that God had chosen me for a purpose, and these trials were His way of communicating with me.

Thus, on a fateful Tuesday night, January 29, 2008, I found myself at a crossroads, torn between the tumult of my mind and the whispered assurances of divine guidance.

Once again, my mom was in Mexico, and I couldn't recall where my kids were, or at least I think I couldn't. I brewed myself a cup of tea for my nerves because I was starting to feel really awful, although in my mind, the tea seemed to make things even worse. Which seemed impossible. I decided to take a shower, hoping it might help. So I went and soaked in the bath because I've always found baths comforting. As I lay there, tears streamed down my face uncontrollably, like a baby crying, like I'd never cried before. I felt utterly hollow inside, shattered, adrift; I embodied every negative emotion imaginable. I longed for a different life, one with my kids, but I didn't know how to attain it. I yearned for the love, attention, and approval I had never received. I had felt so lost for practically my entire life. I needed God, yet I had no idea how to mend myself or my circumstances.

As I bowed my head, it felt as though God began to unravel my life before me like a movie, showing me every moment. This wasn't a dream; it was real life. It was a supernatural encounter—I knew God understood my heart and recognized how much I needed Him. He understood my struggles, my desperate battle against the internal demons consuming me. Afterward, as I rose from the water and reached for my towel, I sensed my grandma's presence so strongly. How did I know it was her? Because I just knew, without a shadow of doubt. I burst into tears once more, and then, it felt as though something washed over me, granting me a sliver of peace. I stepped out of the bath, bewildered. Was I losing my mind? I began texting my sisters, convinced that Grandma had been there. I was always a bit of a rebel back then, and while I had fears, I wasn't usually a nervous wreck like that, so everyone was taken aback.

As days passed, I realized I needed to speak to a priest; this was all too much, and I didn't understand what was happening. I made my way to the church, a place I'd never visited before. I went to the little houses where the priests reside and knocked on the door. Someone answered—I still remember Padre Francisco. "What's wrong?" he asked.

"I think I'm losing my mind!" I exclaimed. He emerged, and we talked for a while. Then he said something that struck me: "God has assigned someone to watch over you from heaven." And in that moment, I knew—it was my grandma. He made the sign of the cross on my forehead after I confessed my wrongdoings and sins, and with that gesture, a wave of peace washed over me, and everything seemed to dissolve away.

All the confusion, all the chaos swirling in my mind, all the doubts—suddenly, they vanish. What just happened? God had singled me out, chosen me for a purpose, because He had a plan for me. He had a good life for me; He wanted to bless me, to take away my pain, my misery, everything I carried. He wanted my heart.

Thinking back on it, it always fills me with gratitude, makes me feel special. It confirmed to me that God had been watching over me, aware of everything I was enduring. He knew I longed for change, that I needed to transform my life, to find healing, and He came to my rescue.

That's when my journey with God truly began. I won't delve into too much detail, but after that, my heart changed. They said even my voice changed. I began feeling convicted when I did things I shouldn't, when I acted in ways that displeased Him, the Holy Spirit. Then I tried to continue living the same wild, partying, alcoholic life. But I couldn't anymore, and for a while, I was angry because He had chosen me. I asked, "Why didn't You choose someone else?" Ha! That was just the beginning.

I had lost faith in love and marriage, especially after discovering my dad had cheated on my mom. He, whom I believed to be loyal and all. I started believing, and since I couldn't have sex anymore, I devoted myself and surrendered my life to God. I craved the family I never had. They say love is where family is, but I never got to experience that. I desired a small family for my kids, a little home where they could just be kids. Where they could make a mess if they wanted, be loud, have their own space.

As I began attending church and healing, it hasn't been easy, but it's been worth it. I started meeting a lot of people, ladies who reminded me of my mom, offering me a glimpse of maternal love, even if only for a moment. Healing from my mommy issues has been really hard; the more I changed and healed, the meaner she seemed to become. And my dad? He was just there, doing anything to please her because he didn't had anything to say.

I started searching for my own places. I couldn't move farther because my kids needed to walk to school. I once confided in my mom that I didn't want to drink alcohol anymore, that I wanted to be different, that I wanted my kids to grow up in a different environment.

I left, and then I returned. When I came back, she had written me a letter, saying that if I didn't want to drink anymore, then I should leave, questioning why I was still there. Was I betraying my family just because I wanted to be different? That's how I felt. Instead of being happy for me, she was unhappy. I remember I was so hurt; I left and went to my sister's house. I showed her the letter, and I cried while my sister prayed over me. It was a secret that I was mistreated as a child until I was older. Everyone knew; I had uncles and aunts who would defend me. There was Aunt Willi; whenever something happened, I would take my kids and go to her house. She knew that when I said I was spending the night, something had happened. Every time I went, my mom would call her and get her in trouble for having me there. Aunt Willi was afraid of my mom too.

I started serving at retreats, and as I began to heal, I became more confused. The more I got to know God, the more bewildered I became. How could a loving God put me in a home like that? How could a loving God place me in a family that would hurt me? How could a loving God, being the father figure, give me parents who would hurt me for 40 years? Yes, 40 years. I'll share more about that in the upcoming pages.

But despite everything, I loved God. People at church would tell me, "That's the cross you have to carry; it's God's mission and plan for our lives." But I couldn't accept it; it didn't felt right in my spirit, even though I didn't know much. I started looking for a place to move. I prayed for the courage to live. I had no money saved, no furniture. I remember sharing with my friend Jessi from work, and she told me, "God will always provide. When God has a plan for your life, He will ensure that plan comes to fruition, including bringing the people you need to help you and support you. God works through people; He uses them to perform miracles. He uses us, you and me."

I finally found a place; my kids were already preteens. The night I brought them home, I had a panic attack around

1 am. I remember repeating a Bible verse over and over, something like "Do not be afraid, for I am with you," until I fell asleep. After getting my kids, I didn't move for about a month because I was so afraid. Even after I had the keys to my new place, my mom started calling everyone, telling them I was leaving and she would be alone. It was always about her, never about what my kids needed or what I needed. She even once told me, "You're going to kill me if you leave.

It's that false sense of responsibility we feel toward our parents. We're taught to put them first, no matter what, to help them because they're our parents and they raised us, as if we owe them something just for being born. We help them even as they break us, even as we're hurting, lost, and in need of help ourselves. Growing up, I saw other girls having their moms as their best friends, and I knew I would never have that.

Healing also means grieving, grieving for the expectations we have that may never be met. It's like trying to catch the wind—you're chasing after something you'll never catch. Some people change, some don't. That's something we'll never know. Something in my spirit has been telling me that I need to grieve, to let go of those ideas, those expectations. I came to the conclusion that I had to accept my parents, accept my mom, and love them for who they are and what they have to offer. They only knew so much; they did the best they could, and I had to make peace with that.

Behind every hurt person, there's always a hard, sad story. As parents, we're bound to fail no matter what. We do what we think is best, but we'll still fail because we're not perfect. Parenting is the hardest job; as people say, nobody showed us how to do it, there's no manual with instructions. We learn through trial and error. But for me, being a parent is the most rewarding feeling. I've always felt that God gifted me to be a mom, not because I'm perfect, but because it comes naturally. I don't see my kids as a burden, I've never had, or that they take away my time. I don't complain; I do everything with love, and I genuinely enjoy it.

As you get older, you need to learn to re-parent yourself. Within the adult you've become, there's still a broken child, as in my case. I had to nurture that broken child, embrace her, and reassure her that everything would be okay. My mom never once acknowledged what she did; she never once asked for forgiveness. Whenever I tried to broach the subject, she would become defensive and neurotic, so I chose never to bring it up again. I let it go and entrusted it to God. I had to believe that God would provide whatever I needed, that He would fill all those areas in my life that needed healing, love, and care

For a couple of years, I served at church, praying for God to send me the husband I desired. They said to be detailed, to ask for everything I wanted, to be specific, so I did. I prayed for someone like my dad—hardworking, ranchero, with no children. I wanted someone without kids because I didn't want the baggage and drama that often comes with it. I prayed that prayer for a long time, for years, until I realized it wasn't working. There was a time when I thought God was listening to me. In my spirit, I knew God wanted marriage for me; I felt it was part of His plan and purpose for my life.

I was content being single, but sometimes I longed for a companion, someone I could talk to, someone to come home to, to have conversations with, and someone to help me build my little family. After my kids' dad, I never moved in with anyone else. I promised myself and my kids that I wanted to get married in the church. It was crucial for my daughter to see me doing things right, or at least what I believed was right for me. I always tried to set a good example for my kids; I didn't want them to see me with different men or to throw it in my face when they got older. It was always important for me to walk the walk and talk the talk, something like that, haha!

My kids knew I was praying to God for a husband. I remember my son telling me he wanted me to have a boyfriend so I could be happy. Didn't he see me happy? One time, we went to Redbox to rent movies, those red boxes they had at the stores. My kids went to pick out movies, and when they came back, they had a movie for me. The title of the movie was "God, help my mom find a boyfriend," haha! My kids might not remember, but I do. God has always spoken through people, through my kids, and through different experiences.

AWAKENED BY CANCER

Chapter 7

Building a New Family

"Every NO is a YES for me."

- Susana-

W hen I realized that the prayer I was saying to God, asking for the husband I desired, wasn't working, I knew I had to change that up. So, I did. My new prayer became, "God, don't give me what I want, give me what you know I need." And then, boom! He showed up in less than a year. While I prayed, I'd often wonder, "How will I know it's him when I see him? How will I know he's the one?" During my prayers, I felt a whisper in my spirit from God, telling me that I'd recognize him because he would embrace me, and I'd feel like I was home. God and I always had this great communication going on. I could feel it deep within. I delved into books about marriage and communication because I realized I didn't know how to navigate these things in a healthy way; I wanted to learn. I had to, because the way I used to handle relationships wasn't healthy or loving.

I thought I was healed, that I was ready for marriage. I believed that as soon as I found the one, we'd head straight to the altar, straight to the church. When I prayed for the husband I believed God had chosen for me, deep down, I knew he was already in my life, somewhere. I had this friend on Facebook, connected through mutual church friends. He was a single parent, or rather, a co-parent, as I could tell from his posts. One day, I commented on one of his posts, admiring how he was as a father, especially since my own children didn't have a father figure.

We started messaging back and forward, and he eventually asked me why I didn't have a boyfriend, a question I often got asked. When I began attending church regularly, devoting my life to God and serving, I stopped dating. I stopped wasting time with men who weren't right for me. I focused on what God had in mind for me. I got focus on healing and becoming the best version of myself, so when the husband God had for me came along, I'd be ready. Many people questioned me because I remained single for a long time.

I remember a coworker who would tease me, saying I'd end up an old maid. I even recall a husband of one of the church ladies calling me to ask how I managed to stay celibate. It surprised me that someone would even think to ask such a thing, especially a married man. After I shared my testimony in their community about what God had been doing in my life, he reached out. I was astonished that someone could surrender their body to God in that way.

That you could surrender your desires to God. That through fasting and praying, you learn to control the body and strengthen the spirit. When we are driven by our physical urges, we simply give in to what the body demands. But we are more than just our physical desires; we are more than our minds and bodies. We are spirit, and it is in that realm where God resides. Submitting yourself to God means being able to do anything He places in your heart, including remaining celibate. During those years, I experienced the purest form of love. Because when you're not fixated on the body, you're not chasing temporary pleasures. Instead, you get focus on genuine love, on truly getting to know someone from a deeper, more emotional place, because the body and sex distract us from what truly matters. Love isn't merely an emotion or a feeling; it's a choice. Love is commitment. Love is forgiveness. Love is choosing to be with someone, day after day

We had been chatting for a couple of days, but in my heart, I never thought much of it. I wasn't seeking anyone out, as I knew God already had someone in mind for me—I was just patiently waiting for that person to appear. We exchanged messages, and then out of the blue, he invited me to his aunt's house. It was his cousin's birthday and graduation party, just a week after we had started chatting on Facebook. On the day of the party, as I was getting ready, I distinctly remember telling my neighbor, who was a friend of mine, that my life was about to change. I couldn't explain how or why, but I had this strong sense that everything was going to be different after that day. It felt strange, and the memory has stuck with me to this day.

He lived about 50 minutes away, quite a distance. Nevertheless, I got ready and headed to his party. He had extended the invitation, so I thought, why not? I hadn't harbored any expectations or desires beyond friendship. Besides the acquaintances from church, I didn't have many male friends. I trusted him because we attended the same church and had mutual friends. I often saw him at church, always carrying his Bible and wearing a cross, so I thought he looked very Catholic, as my mom would say. And so, on June 5th, 2015, I found myself driving to Anaheim. When

I arrived at his aunt's house, I texted him to let him know I was there, and he came out to greet me.

He later confessed that he didn't think I would actually come. I asked him, "Why would you think that?" I suspect deep down he invited me half-hoping I wouldn't show up— haha! So, he comes to fetch me, and when I arrive, he's the taco man, helping his aunt with the tacos. I remember wearing a red t-shirt. He seemed really shy. He leads me to the backyard and gives me a hug. Oh my goodness, that hug! It was the hug I'd been waiting for. In that moment, I felt like he was the man God had chosen for me. A flurry of thoughts rushed through my mind. But I needed confirmation, so I asked him, "Can you hug me again?" He didn't understand why I asked, but I did. I needed that second hug for confirmation. When he hugged me again, I KNEW. He was the one. But I couldn't say anything to him just yet.

As we talked, he cooked, and I was amazed. I sat down, and he served me food. It was the first time someone had treated me like that. We chatted for a while, and then his daughter arrived. I hadn't realized his oldest daughter was there; she was about 13 years old. We hung out for a bit, but then I had to leave because he had to work at midnight. I mean, who does that? He invites me to a party and then has to work at midnight. So, I had to leave early. He walked me to my car, and as I drove away, he went back inside the house. I was in shock. I remember not being able to sleep all night because I was so shocked.

The next day, I texted him, telling him he was the man I'd been waiting for. Looking back, it was probably quite dramatic and surprising for him because he claims he doesn't remember me saying that at all. Can you imagine meeting someone, and the next day they're telling you that? We hung out one more time, and then he asked me to be his girlfriend. He was super shy. I remember him asking me over the phone. At first, we didn't tell our kids. I didn't want to tell mine; I tried to keep it hidden until I got caught. Kids seem to know everything. It's not that I wanted to deceive them, but as I mentioned earlier, I didn't like introducing men to them. Even though I knew he was the one, I wanted us to be serious before involving the kids. I thought he was ready too. So, we started dating, and right away, I told him about the mission I believed God had for me and that I was celibate, intending to wait until marriage to have sex.

He once told me that I was exaggerating; when we discuss it now, he feels regretful about saying that to me. Pleasing God and being obedient to the calling He had for my life were more important to me than anything else. We began dating, and he would come to my house every weekend or every other weekend. He worked tirelessly, juggling two jobs. He'd work graveyard shifts at one job and then part-time in the afternoons. We would talk when he went to his afternoon job—that was the only time he had to talk to me during the weekdays. I thought he was strong in his faith, seeing him at church regularly, serving, carrying his Bible and a cross. But a couple of months into dating, I realized he didn't truly have a relationship with God. He'd come home from church, complaining about everyone not meeting his expectations.

As the skeletons started to emerge from his closet, I began to question God. I thought, "If this is the man You have for me, then something needs to be changed, because what I'm seeing isn't what You want for me." The more I got to know him, the darker things seemed. I had no idea he had just separated from his wife, nor did I know about the tumultuous relationship he had with her. He seemed to be everywhere and nowhere at the same time. But I never asked him to change; instead, I'd pour out my heart to God.

He seemed to have no life of his own; he worked day and night, hardly slept, and barely made any money. I remember him always wearing the same black shirt and the same Converse sneakers. Things started to get confusing. The more I learned about him and his life, the more perplexing it became. The kids always wore the same clothes. Jocey, in particular, always wore the same black flats and burgundy dress. When I looked at the kids, I saw a reflection of myself in them. Meeting their mom felt like meeting my own mom, which was incredibly difficult for me.

It was hard because I wanted to save them; I wanted to do more for them, to rescue them. It felt like history repeating itself. I started questioning some of her decisions. I couldn't fathom how a mother could choose men or other things over her children. As a single parent for many years, having to raise my own kids alone, I couldn't understand why children with both parents would struggle so much. I told my now-husband that I couldn't marry him at the moment. I explained that he had a lot of issues to address before we could even think about setting a wedding date.

He had a lot of things to work on before we could get more serious. He did propose to me after six months, but I always feel like that proposal didn't really count because he didn't love me like that then, nor was he ready to get married. I had this idea that when I met the one, we'd head straight to the church, both of us ready to commit. After a year of dating, I broke up with him because he still wasn't ready; I gave him the ring back. He was indecisive, not fully committed, and he lied a lot. He even admitted to having a problem with lying. He was being manipulated, and there was nothing I could do about it.

After we broke up, I guess he realized that he did want to be with me, that he did want something serious. That's when we started praying together. I began praying for his soul, seeking help even at church to pray for him, to pray for all the baggage he carried. I remember feeling like there was a spiritual battle raging for his soul whenever I prayed for him. It's etched in my memory like it happened yesterday. I started hearing really negative voices in my head, haunting me.

Then one day, God spoke to my spirit, assuring me that it wasn't me; it was him. That's when I intensified my prayers. Having been manipulated for much of my life, I knew what it looked like. I could recognize lies and control tactics. I think he proposed to me initially because he felt pressured, like he had to please me because I had told him he was the one. But when I realized there was so much work to be done, that we needed time, I decided not to rush things and to take my time.

We started praying, and God started working. He allowed God to help him and to heal him. Deep down, I knew he had been in a marriage or long-term relationship for 14 years that wasn't right for him. That's why I never felt threatened by her. All I ever asked for was respect and honesty. She has always respected me, and to this day, we only talk when necessary.

With God working in him and transforming him, the difference from when I first met him to that point was nothing short of miraculous. There was still a lot of work to do, but I felt it was time to set a date for the wedding. He ended up moving in with me just a couple of months before the wedding so we could save money and pay for it.

There was no way we could manage living in two different places and paying two sets of rent and utilities. Dealing with the kids was still a challenge; he did end up hiring a lawyer and obtaining partial custody. We decided to wait until we were married to pursue full custody. After three years of dating, we decided to tie the knot. I meticulously planned the wedding of my dreams, complete with the dress I had always envisioned. Everything I had ever imagined was coming to life.

After we got married, he continued to have difficulties with his kids. I found myself mediating with their mom, as usual. Once again, I felt like I had to be the savior, the one who fixed everything, because if I didn't do it, who else would? Living with someone truly reveals their character, but even after that, understanding them took time. What I saw on Facebook wasn't reality. He didn't live up to the things he said he would do. He was emotionally absent. When issues arose, he would clam up and refuse to communicate. He could go days without speaking to me or simply turn away and go to sleep.

We decided to bring his two youngest kids to live with us. Now, it was the four kids and us in a small apartment.

We told their mom we would take them for a year so she could focus on herself, her marriage, and seek help. I wanted the kids to be in a safe environment, one where they could receive education and discipline, something they lacked before. I became deeply involved in their lives. Surprisingly, my husband was never available. It was baffling how, with our own abandonment issues, we ended up with partners who were unavailable. It's as if we subconsciously seek out what we expect, perpetuating the pattern in our lives.

I took care of the four kids while working full-time. I handled their education and needs. I remember Jocey crying every single night. It must have been traumatic for her to be separated from her mom and then not have her dad be emotionally expressive or available. At the time, I believed I was doing what was best for them, once again putting everyone else's needs before my own. When it came to my kids, it was just me; when it came to his kids, it was still just me. I was the one dealing with everything, all the time.

Whenever I tried to discuss issues with him regarding his kids, he would shut down and go to sleep. I wondered, where was the man I saw on Facebook, so involved with his kids? Meeting his dad and mom helped me understand why. Our upbringing and family environment shape us as adults and significantly influence the type of parents we become.

If we're not aware, we'll just keep repeating the same patterns. Broken parents raise broken kids, and the cycle goes on until someone becomes conscious enough to break it. We stayed in that tiny apartment for what felt like forever. It was so cramped; we barely had enough space. I couldn't bear the thought of the kids going back because I wanted them to have a different future, a better life. But in taking them in, I forgot that I had my own kids who were still young too.

The problem with being codependent is that the more you do for others, the less you think about your own needs. Spending a lifetime focused on others, never on myself, got me into a lot of trouble. I was always searching for someone to be save, someone to love, but I didn't have that love for myself, nor was I in the right place to give it. What happened to all those years I spent healing and crying? People would tell me, "I don't know how you do it," and

I would reply, "God gave me this love for the kids, so it doesn't feel like a burden." And it's true; God did give me that love for the kids from the moment I met them.

I treated them as if they were my own, buying them the same things I'd buy for my own children. But the problem was when I began to focus solely on giving and doing for others, forgetting about myself once again. I lived like that for a couple of years, overworking myself because I thought I was superwoman. I couldn't see it, but those around me did. They'd tell me, but I was convinced the kids needed me—that I was superwoman and could do it all.

In our culture, and perhaps in others too, it's all too common for moms to worry endlessly and do everything for their kids and husbands, forgetting about themselves in the process. We're taught to love our kids more than we love ourselves, to prioritize everyone else's needs above our own. You always see moms doing everything for everyone else, with no one doing the same for them. But what's wrong with this picture? If we always put ourselves last, if we neglect our own well-being and prioritize others over ourselves, what kind of love are we truly giving our children? Leftovers? We are the first ones to show our kids love, and if they see us neglecting ourselves and always putting ourselves last, they'll learn that this is the way to go.

As they grow into adults, they'll often prioritize their needs last, believing it's acceptable because that's what they witnessed at home. We often perceive self-care as selfish, feeling guilty about doing things for ourselves that bring us joy. Taking time off or treating ourselves seems self-indulgent. Self-love isn't something we're taught; once again, our parents didn't know better, or they would have done better. This cycle only breaks when someone in the family decides to break it.

I always say there are two types of children: those who repeat the same patterns and those who choose to create something different and better. Even today, I have to remind myself that I don't have to constantly do everything for everyone. I don't need to fix everyone or try to save everyone.

Every time I do something for someone, I question myself. I need to make sure that I am doing it for the right reasons and not out of obligation. When I married my husband, I married him along with all of his kids, and I took that commitment seriously. I committed to the marriage and to being a stepmom. I believe that when you marry someone with kids, you need to love those kids as much as you love your spouse or your home. If you don't love the kids like that, then maybe you shouldn't marry that person.

When I met the kids and their mom, the mom reminded me a lot of my own mom in some ways. But seeing her always dressed up with makeup, while the kids wore the same clothes and looked unkempt, made me angry. As a mother, I always believed that before anything else, I am a mom to my kids. Providing them with basic necessities like clothes is essential, especially when the other parent is providing child support. The stepdad wouldn't treat them well. Like I said, I could never prioritize a man over my kids. There were always problems, and one time, one of them called us in the middle of the night. That was the breaking point for me. I'd rather have them with me and deal with the problems myself than have them over there.

I thought I was doing the right thing by fighting for them. I believed that bringing them to my house was the best option. Once again, I found myself being the fixer, the one who always has to solve everything for everyone. I started talking to the mom, trying to convince her that bringing the kids to our house was the best thing to do. I told her it would be temporary, just until she got her life together and sought help for herself. What hurt her the most was the youngest one. More than once, she made me feel like she didn't care about the boy. That was something that deeply hurt me and brought tears to my eyes.

I understood what it was like for your parents to not love you, at least not to show it, because I know our parents love us in their own way. I think she was happy he was here because she had problems with her husband because of him. As parents, sometimes we show more love to one child than to the others. I don't think we do it intentionally, but it happens. Most of the time, we don't even realize it. I spoke to the mom several times, and we gave her an ultimatum. We just wanted the kids to do well in school, to get the support they needed, attention, and for their needs to be met.

I feel that when you feel sorry for yourself, it's easy to feel sorry for someone else. When you feel you can't do something or feel a certain way about yourself, that's how you feel about others. I needed to save myself, and they were there for me to save. I thought my husband was going to be supportive, so I went for it. When you're raised with an absent father, you get involved with people who aren't available. My husband was physically there, but emotionally absent. So the kids moved in with us. First the son, then the daughter. They started going to school here. I didn't realize how far behind Sophia was in school until she moved in with me and started attending classes. She would tell us she never did homework. They were at the mall every single day. School and education weren't important to them. When I brought the kids to live with us, I noticed my husband wasn't supportive. He was always working and never made an effort to get involved in their education. When I would tell him about problems I had with the kids, he would just shut down, go to sleep, and leave me hanging, alone with my thoughts.

I started doing so much to keep the kids busy. I had four kids, a full-time job, and a house to take care of. I took care of their education, discipline, and doctor's visits, even taking Erick to therapy. I started doing too much. I went from having my little family of three to a family of six. I had been overworked and overstressed most of my life, so

I didn't see it. Would I do it again? Probably not. The kids have their parents, and the parents need to do their job. If they don't, it's not on me. I'm not responsible. I was supposed to be the stepmom, the support, but I took on being the mom and more. No one told me to do it. No one told me I was responsible for it. It was me again, thinking I had to fix and help everyone.

The codependency. Then I sent the oldest back and only kept the younger one, and then they were separated. It was horrible. Thanks to that experience, I believe we are all in a better place now. I think we all learned from it. I still have to remind myself at times that certain things are not for me to worry about. I'm always talking to myself, reminding myself what my priorities are and what I'm really responsible for. After a couple of years of having both of them, and because of all the stress I was carrying, mostly because I thought I was carrying the whole load myself, I started feeling really stressed out. I started doubting myself.

Was this really the right thing to do? Was this really the best thing for all of us involved? What about my kids? There was so much going through my head. People would tell me that I was crazy. People would tell me that they wouldn't do what I am doing. I did it from a place of love; I genuinely love the kids. But the extra work and thinking that I had to fix everything and help them, was that really something I was responsible for? I don't think so.

Susana Barrios

Chapter 8

2020 — This is the reason I wrote this book

"We think we have time, but in reality we don't; today is all we have..."

- Susana-

Towards the end of 2019, transitioning into 2020, I found myself crying every night. But I didn't understand why. I think I was handling with too much stress. I vividly recall telling my husband how unhappy I felt, how much I needed his support with his kids, yet I never seemed to receive it. I've always been a positive person; it's been one of my shields. So, even when something was wrong, I'd try to remain positive and focus on the bright side. But sometimes, that positivity masks your true feelings and what's really happening inside. I didn't realize I had lost myself for so long — lost in the process of caring for the kids. I gave so much that I left myself empty. I was doing so much, but as I've always been incredibly busy and in survival mode,

I failed to see it. From the bottom of my heart, I tried to give the kids the best, though it wasn't always perfect. My intentions were good. I'd still work out and walk about 5 miles a day. But looking back, I don't think I enjoyed it; I remember always feeling anxious. Instead of walking to relax or feel better, I walked to escape because of my anxiety. We were living in a small apartment at the time — six of us in a cramped two-bedroom space. I remember how crowded and stifling it was. My point is, you can't give more to others than you give to yourself because if you do it, you'll lose yourself.

I cried every night; I was simply exhausted. Tears would just flow. I felt as if I was going to die, literally. It was like falling into a black hole, and the more I struggled to climb out, the me deeper I sank into it.

Why is it that when we grow up with unavailable parents, we end up marrying someone similar? Perhaps, I married the wrong person, but there were things we should have handled differently. Different choices, different plans, and me learning to let go, not trying to control everything and everyone.

January 1st, 2020 arrived, a year that will be etched in our memories forever. I recall preparing for the New Year's festivities with a sense of anticipation; I've always believed the best is yet to come. I spent New Year's Eve at my cousin's house, but it was a strangely off night—filled with drama and toxicity. It wasn't until my family stopped talking to me that I realized how toxic they were; a realization I've come to appreciate with time. I had already been focused on breaking the cycles of toxicity. When you're afraid of losing people or upsetting them, you tolerate a lot of nonsense—nonsense you may not even see because survival has been your norm, and it's all you know, so you don't realize it's wrong. I have many unpleasant memories of family members. Over time, I learned that blood doesn't define family; family is made up of those who love and care for me, those who have been there when I needed them most.

In 2020, we had big plans. I was on the verge of securing a permanent job, and we were getting ready to buy our first house. I had been manifesting so many things, declaring that this was going to be "the year"! I had everything mapped out, or so I thought. I was healthy—at least, that's what I believed. By healthy, I mean physically fit. I wanted my kids to have a comfortable living space.

We often think we control time, that we can make plans. We forget to live in the present moment and fail to acknowledge that things can change overnight. Then came February, and the Covid virus began its rampage. It was a frightening time, like living in a surreal movie — a scenario none of us had experienced before. The virus spread rapidly. I was working at the school district, and on March 13th, 2020, they decided to shut down the schools and all district offices. As a substitute, I was laid off after nearly twenty years of continuous work. I wondered, "What am I going to do with myself? How will I fill my time?" Anxiety started creeping in. It wasn't about the money; I was receiving unemployment benefits, which were substantial. I used to walk six miles every day, but looking back, it didn't calm me; it heightened my anxiety. I couldn't stay still; I couldn't relax. I never knew how to relax. I was always keeping myself busy. When you dislike your reality, you tend to escape from it. And how do you escape? By keeping yourself distracted.

There went my chance at a permanent job. It seemed like it was slipping away for good. I needed stability, something with benefits. Without medical insurance, I felt vulnerable. I had never been without it before. My biggest fear had always been falling ill without coverage.

Luckily, my husband didn't lose his job. My daughter was in San Diego. Everywhere you turned, all you heard about was Covid—how people were dying, how rapidly it was spreading, and how terrifying it had become.

I remember being terribly ill around my birthday, although I didn't realize it was Covid until months later when they identified the symptoms. Without insurance, my sister provided me with medication, even her inhaler. It reminded me of our childhood when we had no medical insurance. We used to borrow our cousin's insurance and had to pretend our uncles were our parents because we didn't have any documentation at the time. We got our papers when we were around 12. Looking back, how did we manage back then without insurance when I was frequently falling ill?

By April, I was still crying at night—now that I recall, it was only at night. I felt like there was something wrong with me, but I couldn't pinpoint what it was. I remember staying up late every night. One thing I realized during that time was that I thrived on structure and routine. Without them, I felt scattered. When I was working, I had a routine. But being home, I was all over the place—not eating right, not sleeping right. I was a mess!

One night, as I lay in bed around eleven, for some reason, I decided to do a self-check of my breasts. I had never done it before; I always found it daunting. While examining my right breast, I felt a lump. I remember that moment vividly. I was shocked but not scared. I immediately turned to YouTube to learn how to perform self-exams. It was the only lump I felt—a hard one, about the size of a bean. It didn't felt normal, but I didn't think much of it. Of course, I never imagined it could be something serious. Remember, I had no insurance.

As soon as I woke up, I immediately called a nearby clinic where I had been before and knew they offered free check-ups. I scheduled a pap smear appointment; back then, they would also check your breasts during a pap smear. I had to find a way to get checked because I didn't have any money to pay otherwise. They gave me an appointment for the following Friday. I didn't think much of it; I just knew it wasn't normal to have a lump there. About five years prior, I had my first mammogram, and everything was fine. I think that's why I wasn't overly concerned. Or maybe you just don't think anything of it, especially when cancer isn't common in your family.

The days passed, and it was time for the appointment. In 2020, due to Covid, no one could accompany you anywhere, especially to doctors' appointments or hospitals. They were very strict, especially because Covid was just starting, and they were still figuring things out. The day of my appointment arrived. After the pap smear, I asked the doctor to check my breast. I remember as soon as she examined it, she felt something abnormal and said I needed to get a mammogram ASAP. I worried not about having anything wrong, but about how much I was going to pay for it. Due to Covid, many places offering free check-ups were closed. I found one, but I had to pay $500.00 upfront just for the deposit. Ugh, I hate mammograms.

I went for the mammogram, got the exams done, and they told me to wait about two weeks for the results. Typically, the waiting game is the hardest; there's always fear about what the results might say. In my case, I wasn't afraid, and cancer never crossed my mind. It's like hearing about things happening to others but never imagining it happening to you.

When I returned to the clinic, the doctor immediately said it was time for a biopsy, something I had never considered. It's when they take a sample from the lump and send it to the lab to determine if it's malignant or benign. Again, as she talked to me about the biopsy, I didn't think much of it. I never thought I would have something wrong. The day arrived, and I went for the biopsy.

I went by myself; again, I had to pay a big amount of money. I didn't expect it to be that challenging, and it was a bit painful. I remember when I got back to my car after the exam, tears started streaming down my face. My husband didn't go with me, and even my sister was upset with him for letting me go alone. It was a new experience for me, and we didn't think much of it. Due to Covid, everywhere was strict, especially hospitals and clinics. I had to go alone because no one could accompany me. Those were scary times during Covid, almost like being in a movie. I wonder if all the attention on Covid made me less worried about my own situation.

After the biopsy, I had to wait up to two weeks for the results. I never once had negative thoughts. I carried on with my life as if nothing was happening, as if I wasn't waiting for any results, especially from a biopsy. Waiting for results is always nerve-wracking, especially now that cancer seems to be so prevalent. It's like cancer has become as common as cholesterol, something you hear about every day. It's affecting people of all ages—kids, teens, older adults, and just about anyone.

That year wasn't just about Covid; it felt like Covid came to impact our lives so we could reflect, be grateful, and reevaluate our life choices. It worked as a reminder that things can change in the blink of an eye. We may think we have everything under control and our lives planned out with goals, but in reality, we never truly know. There's a saying that goes, "If you want to make God laugh, tell him your plans."

I believe this is why it's always crucial to prioritize God in everything we do or plan because He is the only one who truly knows what's best and what the future holds. I recall forgetting about God; He's always been like my best friend, and I've generally been close to Him. Sometimes, amidst our busy lives and routines, we tend to overlook Him, forgetting that we exist because of Him and for Him. I got swept up in my stress, in my bustling life, and in my own strength, thinking I could handle it all, fix it all, without realizing I was deceiving myself.

That year, I was definitely going through something; it's as if the stress finally caught up to me—unemployment, uncertainty, constant anxiety, nights filled with tears. I was drained, utterly exhausted. When I say "done," I mean done with the stress. Throughout my life, I've cared for others, always striving to please them, but in the process, I lost myself.

On the afternoon of May 8th, 2020, I received a call from the clinic asking me to come in as soon as possible. I told them I was on my way since I practically lived across the street. After the call, I wondered, "Why are they calling me? Why do they want me to come in?" I was still awaiting the biopsy results, but I didn't think much of it. I know it might sound repetitive, but I truly never dwelled on negative thoughts. However, I do remember when people found out I was getting a biopsy, they would reassure me, saying, "Don't worry, it's probably nothing." Yet, something inside me didn't quite agree with that notion, although deep down, I always felt that, regardless of the outcome, I would be okay.

I feel that a part of me sensed something was amiss, call it my spirit or gut feeling, whatever you like. God always prepares you, which is why it's crucial to take the time to be with ourselves, to listen to God, but most importantly, to listen to our bodies.

So, when they called me, I went ahead and went. I remember that day vividly, as if it were yesterday. It was the day that changed my life forever, the day I got the news no one wants to hear. I went alone because of Covid; no one could go with me, and I didn't think I needed anyone. Both my kids were at home; I told them the doctor had called and wanted to see me, so they knew where I was headed. While they knew I was waiting for results, I didn't mention the specifics to them because I wasn't sure why the doctor had called, in fact, they didn't say much over the phone. Interestingly, my daughter already had a feeling I might have cancer, a thought that never crossed my mind. Most people fear cancer when facing a biopsy. I didn't, because I never imagined cancer could happen to me. We never think it will knock on our doors.

I drove to the clinic, just a block away, one of those clinics where you use a green card for free women's exams because I had no insurance at the time. I walked to the door, stepped in, and signed my name. I remember exactly what I was wearing. I sat down and waited for the doctor to call my name. A few minutes later, they called me. As I approached the door where the doctor awaited, the first thing she asked was, "Did someone come with you?" Why would she ask that? Why inquire about a companion when it's during Covid, and no one can accompany you? Her question struck me; I never thought of anything specific, but I knew they were asking for a reason. I entered the room, took a seat; it was so cold, and I was in jeans shorts. I waited for the doctor. Fast forward, ever since then, I developed PTSD whenever I visit doctors and have to wait in rooms. Haha.

The doctor walked in; I remember she was a very kind young lady dressed in white. As she approached me, the only thing I recall her saying is, "I am sorry." When those words left her lips, my heart plummeted. I had seen scenes like this in movies, shows and soap operas, but now it was real life, happening to me. I was facing this news all alone. Tears welled up in my eyes. It felt surreal, like I was caught between reality and a dream. Have you ever experienced that sensation where you're unsure if you're dreaming or awake, trying to decipher reality from illusion? Moments like this don't hit you immediately; they take time to process. So, upon receiving the news, I broke down in tears. The visit with the doctor was brief. I stepped outside, and there were some bricks by the clinic. I sat down, attempting to grasp what had just happened.

I remember texting my coach, informing her of my cancer diagnosis. Then, I messaged my closest friend, the one I trust everything in, and shared that the biopsy came back positive. I recall her asking if she should come over, but I couldn't bring myself to respond. My mind was consumed with thoughts of my children, knowing I had to return home and break the news to them. I called my husband; he was on his way to his second job, or maybe I texted him, I can't quite recall, asking him to come home. Without hesitation, he complied. Meanwhile, my sister was returning from Vegas. I texted her, casually mentioning that I had cancer, almost as if it were a common cold.

It felt like an out-of-body experience, as if I was there, but not fully present. Driving back home, I found my kids waiting for me, my daughter already in tears. As I entered, I gathered them and shared the news: the tests had come back positive; I had cancer. Despite the gravity of the situation, I reassured them, telling them that this was something permitted by God because there was a lesson to be learned from it. I emphasized that the word "cancer" would not be spoken of again in our home.

This will test our faith, but everything will be fine. When something like this happens to a family member, it doesn't just affect the individual going through it; it impacts the entire family. Each person involved will have their own unique experience and way of coping. When my husband came home, I shared the news with him, and he started crying. I offered him the same reassurance I gave to my kids. Later, my sisters stopped by after returning from Vegas, and they too were in tears. They expected to find me devastated, but strangely, I was at peace.

I was acting as though nothing was happening, but the reality hadn't fully sunk in yet. I didn't immediately tell my parents; I tried to keep it to myself as much as possible. However, I couldn't hide it for long, especially when my mom kept asking about the biopsy results. Moms always seem to have a sense when something's wrong. The doctor was going to refer me to Arrowhead Hospital, to their oncology department. My grandpa had passed away because of stomach cancer, and I vividly remembered watching him suffer slowly and painfully. That experience had always linked cancer in my mind to pain and suffering, particularly with chemotherapy.

I recall him becoming terribly sick from the treatment, so I associated chemotherapy with his decline in health and how weak it made him. Although my memories of his illness are blurry, we tend to attach words to experiences or associate experiences with feelings. It's not just what happens, but how we felt during those moments. Our bodies store these memories, and when something similar occurs, it's as if we're reliving those moments all over again. Oncology called me right away. Suddenly, I found myself going to the doctor's office three or four times a week for several months. Everything was happening so rapidly that I felt like I couldn't keep up. Not only that, but I had to face it all alone due to the restrictions of COVID-19; no one could accompany me.

I received my diagnosis in May, and by June, I was already undergoing a mastectomy. It was a choice between a mastectomy or radiation, so I opted for the surgery. The hospitals were full, bustling with COVID-19 patients. It felt surreal, like being in a movie, everyone clad in COVID uniforms to prevent infection, and no visitors allowed. It was a profoundly lonely experience. Whenever fear gripped me, I turned to prayer, imagining Jesus embracing me, comforting me, and soothing my anxiety. That became my go-to prayer. As I prepared for surgery, I couldn't help but think about women undergoing surgery for breast augmentation while I was having mine removed—quite the contrast.

On the day of the surgery, two nurses wearing breast cancer pins held my hands. How was it that someone who always felt so alone was going through this diagnostic alone? Did I bring this upon myself? Was this part of God's plan? I made up my mind to focus on one thing: healing. Healing from the root causes of cancer, addressing unresolved trauma, and focusing on my spiritual and emotional well-being. From the start of my journey, I chose to fix my gaze on God and myself. I had a choice: to complain or to view this as an opportunity for deeper reliance on God instead of people. We always have a choice.

It's not about what happens to us, but how we respond to it. Upon receiving my diagnosis, knowing what lay ahead, I started walking and exercising vigorously. I felt the need to prepare my body, knowing I wouldn't be able to exercise for a long time post-surgery. I went on hikes, visited waterfalls, and spent time at Malibu Beach, immersing myself in nature. Mentally, I braced myself for the challenges ahead, seeking peace and strength from God. Throughout it all, I embraced the process without complaint. It's okay to complain; God understands our hearts, and as imperfect humans, we need to acknowledge and express our feelings without judgment. Society often discourages us from expressing our emotions, leading us to second-guess ourselves or worrying about others' reactions when we do. I simply wanted to be sick in peace, to heal, to cry, and to allow myself to be vulnerable for once. Throughout my life, I've always been strong—out of necessity, I became like a rock.

So, now I was attempting to be vulnerable, allowing myself to feel, to acknowledge that I don't always have to be the strong one. It's okay to cry, it's okay to yearn for someone to take care of you, like your family, husband, and kids. After the mastectomy, looking at myself in the mirror was incredibly challenging because of how unsightly the scar was. I dubbed it "the shark bite" because it resembled the aftermath of a shark attack. Why a shark? I don't know, haha! I distinctly recall the first time I put on a shirt and felt so disfigured because it was painfully obvious that I only had one breast. When my mom heard me, she burst into tears.

Surprisingly, telling my parents the news wasn't as difficult as I had anticipated. Parents possess a strength that defines understanding. We're stronger than we realize, and God always provides us with strength when we need it most. My main concern and focus were my kids because I am their everything. No one will ever love them the way I do. Additionally, I believe that if God is going to take you, it's because He already has a plan for your kids and family. As everything started unfolding, I found myself sitting outside, crying, and having a heart-to-heart with God. I confessed that I didn't like who I was; I felt so hardened, as if I had no emotions. I had been trying to change for so long—attending church, fasting, praying, going on retreats, and much more. I pleaded with Him, asking that if He was going to leave me here, He would change me; otherwise, He should take me. I was placing all my trust in Him. Every time I shed tears during my healing journey—funny how I called it a healing journey despite going through a cancer treatment —it felt as though my body was getting weaker, but my spirit was growing stronger.

It's all about focus and perspective. I don't expect anyone to feel or interpret things as I did, nor should we compare our journeys to others'. Your story is unique, and you should embrace it and cherish it. Having only one breast was new territory for me, so I had to come to terms with my new body, my new reality. Accepting what I saw in the mirror took me a considerable amount of time. Eventually, I knew I would get there, but I granted myself grace. I allowed myself to experience my emotions and take things at my own pace. I wasn't rushing it. You don't truly appreciate your body until you lose a part of it. I had always complained about how large my breasts were, and look at me now.

Undergoing a mastectomy was incredibly painful; I relied heavily on assistance, thankfully from my husband, who became my personal caregiver. Sleeping almost upright in a recliner became the norm. We had to adapt to these changes and make necessary adjustments to aid in my recovery and ensure my comfort. After the mastectomy, Oncology declared me healed, stating that the cancer had been removed along with my breast. In my mind, I had always been healed. You see, I've never put much stock in what doctors say.

The one and only authority is God; ultimately, it's up to Him to allow anything. Doctors are limited by what they've learned in school, but God's knowledge is boundless. When we put too much emphasis on what doctors say, it can be discouraging and detrimental to our well-being. A positive mindset, especially during times like this, can only come from above. Following my surgery, I was discharged home the same day. Due to Covid, extended stays at the hospital weren't an option. I had drains, and my husband took on the task of cleaning and measuring them. It was quite unpleasant; there were times when they would open, causing blood to spill everywhere. A spacer was inserted at the site of my mastectomy to stretch my skin and make room for the implant. It was excruciating. For six months, I couldn't sleep on my stomach; any movement felt like my skin was being scraped raw. It was agonizing.

In June of 2020, Oncology called to reschedule my chemotherapy infusions for a later date. Everything was happening so rapidly; I barely had time to react. At this point, chemotherapy was merely a precautionary measure, aimed at preventing the cancer from returning. In reality, no one knows for sure. While writing this book, I had a scare, but it turned out to be nothing. Still, a small voice in the back of my mind whispers, "What if it comes back?" I'd never received so many flowers in my life as I did during this time. The sudden influx of attention was almost uncomfortable for someone unaccustomed to it. Here I was, falling ill once again, and suddenly everyone was showering me with attention.

My husband drove me to my first chemotherapy infusion. Once again, it was during Covid, and I had to go in alone. It was just me and God. I wanted to maintain the facade that everything was okay, that I wasn't scared. Pretending had been my modus operandi throughout my life, always projecting strength even when I felt weak inside. I even posted on Snapchat, pretending I was at a spa because I brought along things to keep me occupied. Pretending, pretending, pretending. Strength had always been my default setting; I didn't know how to be anything else. We all wear masks, using them as our coping mechanisms. Behind those masks, we hide. That's why I became codependent, always trying to save everyone else to avoid facing my own life. And there I was, doing exactly that.

As they inserted the needle into my hand to start the chemotherapy, I observed everyone around me. I heard a woman talking about how her cancer had spread throughout her body. Another lady asked the doctor if she was going to die. In that room, you see people fighting for their lives, others who know their time is limited. Besides it all, you have to stay strong, to remain positive. You can't let what you witness bring you down; it's all in the mind. As the chemotherapy began coursing through my body, my hand grew cold to the point where they had to provide warm clothes. It was the oddest sensation.

I could feel the medication traveling up, and as it reached my chest, I started to react. I couldn't breathe; it felt like I was underwater, watching my blood pressure rise. I called out to the nurses while simultaneously praying to God, begging for help, pleading not to die. The nurses rushed to my aid, removing everything and covering me with a curtain. I was in tears, terrified at the thought of dying. I couldn't help but wonder, what goes through the minds of those who are facing death? My children were my constant concern throughout the ordeal. After a while, they administered Benadryl and resumed the chemotherapy.

My hair, once long and cherished, was destined to fall out after the first chemotherapy session. I had prayed for God's help to see myself with love and compassion once I lost my hair. It was a blow; my hair meant everything to me. I used to take such pleasure in styling it each morning.

God had halted my life; cancer had come to heal me, to address the many wounds I carried. It was a time for change; I couldn't continue living as I had. Doing so would miss the point entirely. It was just me and God, seeking answers within. Everything we need and search for lies within ourselves, yet we seldom take the time to listen or look within.

That's why we find ourselves lost and in suffering. When cancer paid a visit, I had to rediscover my voice, one I had let go silent. I can't pinpoint when or why. The moment I stopped advocating for myself, I lost sight of who I was. Now, I had to reclaim that person; this journey was about me, my process, and my healing. Even after my first chemotherapy session, I still had my two stepkids to care for. I did everything I thought was right for them at the time. But now, it was time to send them back to their mom. I needed to prioritize taking care of myself, to focus on me for once.

About a week after my first chemo, my hair began to fall out. Before I went completely bald, I asked my husband to shave it off. It wasn't a difficult decision for me; when survival is your focus, your hair becomes the least of your worries. And just like that, I became an official cancer patient. After that initial round of chemo, my body reacted in so many ways. It was brutal; my skin darkened, and everything started to taste metallic, like being pregnant with morning sickness. I was making changes, and the first step was sending the kids back to their mom. My husband disagreed, but since he hadn't been involved in helping, his opinion didn't hold weight. We argued; he wanted them to stay, but I had to prioritize myself. Their mom was young and healthy, while I was growing weaker and sicker. I knew my stepdaughter wanted to be with her mom, and vice versa. I sent my stepson back first, and later in the year, my stepdaughter. Everything I did came from a place of love, but I couldn't keep doing it. My cup was empty.

I was scheduled for a total of six rounds of chemo, spaced three weeks apart. The first week after each session was always the toughest. Just as I was recovering, it was time for the next round. My body grew weaker with each passing treatment, and toward the end, I experienced both nausea and vomiting simultaneously. But amidst it all, my spirit grew stronger. I began to notice a pattern: here I was, like a child, getting sick and receiving attention. How did I end up here? How did I lose myself while helping others? I prayed, I wrote, and I stayed awake at night, pondering.

What if this was it? What if my time was up? With chemotherapy and Covid, so many things could go wrong. The nights were the hardest; I started taking prescribed medication to help me sleep.

With this process and everything happening with Covid, it became incredibly difficult. Nights were especially challenging, anxiety creeping in. Yet, amidst it all, I found solace in worship. How could someone undergoing such a trial worship God? His Holy Spirit enveloped me, bringing joy and peace throughout. God was shaping me, setting me free from expectations, codependency, and other burdens. I came to realize I didn't need anyone else's attention; I needed my own. I needed to be present for myself. The inner child within me yearned for the love and attention she never received. We cling to hope, hoping one day for the family we wished we had in childhood. In this process, I had to grieve those expectations, the image of the parents I thought I needed but would never have. I learned to be grateful for what they could offer at the time, holding onto the good and letting go of the hurtful.

God began revealing many truths to me, ones I hadn't seen before. I started affirming to myself that I was in a safe place, loved, and beautiful because God intended it. It was His plan, not anyone else's. As time passed, I grew weaker, spending days sleeping, only waking to eat or visit the doctor. Yet in my mind, I pictured myself healed in the future. Breakthroughs came, understanding dawned. I began to feel and know that I was enough, that through God, I had everything I needed. Looking in the mirror, seeing my altered appearance—no breast, no hair—might have seemed defeat, but I had never felt stronger or more resolute. I spoke to myself in the mirror, reminding myself I wasn't a victim, that I had the power to create the life I desired. Cancer was breaking me, but with it came the breaking of dysfunctional beliefs, thoughts, and habits that no longer served me.

I began to embrace my humanity, allowing myself to feel, see, and be more vulnerable. During this process, my relationship with my kids flourished. I became more present, and our communication improved daily. I learned that you can't give what you don't have, and to help your kids, you must first help yourself. While we often focus on getting help for our children, the key lies in helping ourselves first; then, everything falls into place. This journey was about self-help, healing, shedding tears, talking to God, and rebuilding myself after feeling broken. Isolated for six months due to Covid, I had ample time for self-reflection.

Each day during chemotherapy felt like a victory. Gratefulness filled my nights, acknowledging that I had made it through another day. I could only live one day at a time; the future seemed too distant and overwhelming. I cherished the second chance God had given me. Cancer became a wake-up call. Without it, I might have become bitter and unhappy. Cancer awakened something within me; the light that had been dimmed throughout my life finally shone. I began to love myself, accepting the person I saw in the mirror with all my strengths and weaknesses. I appreciated who I was becoming.

Even now, I wake up grateful for this new opportunity, thanking God not just every day but every second for allowing Cancer to come and impart these valuable lessons. They say our bodies speak what we don't express in sickness. Not everyone gets cancer, so why me? I tried to make the best of this process, opening up to the lessons life wanted to teach me, attempting to heal and uncover the root causes. Some answers may remain elusive, but I endeavored to make the best of the situation.

After an experience like this, many things that once mattered lose their significance. Focus shifts, and you begin to choose your battles rather than having battles choose you. I became selective about who had access to me, and my circle grew smaller. It became about quality over quantity. It felt like a rebirth, as if everything before Cancer didn't count. Life paused for a moment, giving me a chance to be born again into a better place with better choices. I felt free—free to be myself, free to say yes or no without feeling guilty.

Free to choose what I want for myself, not for anyone else. It's like seeing the world through a different lens. It's akin to having a near-death experience and returning—to do the things you didn't do before, to travel, to find happiness. Sitting outside, basking in nature, enjoying the simple act of breathing, feeling that you're truly living, not merely surviving. It's waking up each day and choosing happiness, making the most of every moment. It's living one day at a time. I began to rebuild my relationship with God, returning to church, back to the one constant presence throughout my entire journey.

While writing this book, I experienced another experience. I saw cancer everywhere—in shows, movies, and everything around me. Something inside me still feared that cancer could return. I needed more than just prayers; I needed to be set free from this fear, this disease, from anything that could instill fear and open the door to this terrible thing. I returned to The Way World Outreach, the only place where I truly felt the love of God, where I felt at home, where I felt I belonged. In my spirit, I felt led to go there specifically; God had something for me. I had been praying for deliverance. I knew it wasn't God's plan for me to live in fear, nor is it for anyone. We didn't come into this world to suffer, to be sick, or to live in constant fear. Fear is learned; sickness comes with time, and we lose ourselves in the process of life.

There is a power greater than us, and we all must believe in that higher power. For me, it's always been and will always be God. We can't do it alone; we were not meant to. We lose hope when we stop holding onto that belief, when we stop believing in help, purpose, and that the best is yet to come. At least for me, believing in God, holding onto hope, and praying for strength has always worked. I wouldn't be here today writing this book without Him. He didn't plan for my life to be easy, but He did allow it. He gave me purpose; He turned my pain into power, my mess into a blessing. Now, I have a story to tell, a purpose behind everything that has happened to me. I couldn't sit here and have so many stories, share the many blessings, the countless opportunities He has given me through trials, pain, and sickness to bless me. Because even though it's not part of His plan, He can use anything that happens to us for our good.

No matter what it is, no matter how much it hurts. I was obedient, so I started going to church, seeking deliverance. I believe that some sicknesses enter in our bodies to hinder the blessings that God has for us. Why is it that, no matter what you do, will you still get sick? No matter how much faith you have, fear still wants to control your life. When something is stronger than you, it's time for us to turn to Him, to seek Him, and to ask Him to set us free.

I was at service, and for some reason, I had been bawling my eyes out. I had been crying so much, even surprising myself because in my head, there was no reason. It was the Holy Spirit that had touched me, that was trying to set me free. The pastor was preaching about sickness that day, and on the screen, they had Cancer listed as one of them. I remember that when I saw that word, it did something in my spirit. I started crying even more. I recall the pastor's voice sounding distant at times, as if it would fade in and out.

I knew in my heart that I was there because I needed prayer, I needed deliverance. I needed that fear of cancer coming back to leave my life because I refused to live in fear. I knew then, as I do now, that God's plan is not for us to live like that. Fear does not come from God; it comes from the devil. The devil is here to steal, kill, and destroy. He wants to steal the life God has planned for you. He wants you discouraged, fearful, and sick. He knows you're a threat to him because God has anointed you with purpose, power, and a story that needs to be told. A story that will be a blessing and will bring breakthrough to people who may have had similar experiences or are going through similar things.

As the pastor closed the service in prayer, I was still crying, crying for help, crying for a prayer, for something powerful that would deliver me from this fear that was stealing my peace. The pastor began calling people to the altar, saying if you need God's love, if you need this or that, come to the front for prayer. In my head, I was thinking, "No, I don't need that. I need deliverance." I kept crying,

141

standing in front of my seat. I was in the first row because I liked to sit in the front; if I sat in the back, I'd get easily distracted. People tend to talk a lot during service, and that's something I can't stand.

People kept walking to the front for prayer, and Pastor Marco handed the microphone to another pastor before leaving. There I was, still crying, telling myself that if God really wanted me at the front, He would call me. How? I didn't know. That's always been my faith—God can make things happen. It's not for us to figure out how, but to be still and know that He is God. I trusted that He would make it happen; I just needed to have faith. Faith is believing in the unknown, believing in things that we don't see but already have. In the spirit, they already exist.

As Pastor Marco was leaving the stage, he suddenly walked back. He asked for the microphone and said, "If there's someone here that needs prayer for Cancer, come to the front." I was shocked. I almost wanted to yell out, "That's me!" When he said that, I walked to the front. It was the answer to my prayer and my longing for deliverance. When I reached the altar, a beautiful young lady started praying for me. I remember her face vividly, as if it were yesterday—a face I'll never forget. I got on my knees and began praying and crying, pleading with God to deliver me, to set me free. In my spirit, I felt led to pray for deliverance from cancer.

As she prayed for me, I felt resistance—a struggle as if something inside me wanted to come out but couldn't. As she continued praying, I felt as if no one else existed, as if it were just the two of us in the church, and everyone else had already gone. Her prayers grew more powerful, and I felt as if I had left my body, watching myself from the outside. The tears flowed, and suddenly, a loud yell burst from my body. It felt as though cancer had left my body. After that prayer, I felt so relieved, as if a heavy weight had been lifted off my shoulders. The fear that had haunted me no longer had a hold on me. I had been set free.

Fear will always be there; we are human, flesh, and imperfect. It wouldn't be normal for me not to feel fear. Fear reminds me of my humanity, reminding me that I need God all the time, every day, every second. Despite the fear of "What if cancer comes back?" I choose faith over fear. God knows my heart; He has a plan for me, a purpose greater than I can imagine. Every time fear creeps in, I choose to have faith. I choose to believe that if God has set me free, then I am free indeed.

After cancer, my life has completely changed. I feel as though I've been reborn, given a second chance at life—a chance I don't want to squander. I'm grateful every time I wake up. Looking back, especially at the pictures from when I was going through chemotherapy, fills me with gratitude. Sometimes it feels like it wasn't even me, like it was someone else going through that ordeal. During that time, I aged significantly. I looked old, sick, and my body seemed so fragile. But God used that to heal me, to bring me back to life, to awaken me. Because that's who God is: A God of miracles, deliverance, mercy, and above all, love. He can use anything in your life for your good. Something that seems so painful and tragic can be turned into a beautiful story. Your pain can become your power. Your story can bless others, inspire hope, and brighten someone's life. It's not what we do during pain, but who we become in the process. It's when our faith is tested that we truly see where we stand.

Cancer came to awaken me; I had been asleep for so long. After cancer, I started truly living. I began to appreciate every day, grateful for each morning I opened my eyes. I landed the job I'd been wanting, finally reaching a point where I enjoy who I am, where I've accepted myself, and where I have a job I love. What changed? I started believing in myself, chasing opportunities that came my way. I stopped wasting time. In just two years, I doubled my income. I traveled to Mexico for the first time. My relationship with my husband and kids flourished. Now, I'm in a place in my life where I feel full, seen, heard, and understood—by myself. Physically, I'm at my strongest; I'm not just healthy, I'm strong.

When she looked in the mirror and saw herself without hair, eyelashes, or a breast, she realized she had lost many things but had found herself. Everything else was just a part of her body, not who she was. She had to lose herself to rediscover who she truly was.

That's when life truly began...

Farewell

I wrote this book with deep respect for all those involved. I harbor no grudges, no lingering negativity towards anyone. I have forgiven and moved forward, holding nothing but gratitude in my heart. Every person that gets in our lives is to impart a lesson, and we are all on a journey towards a better place. Thank you, God. I hope that my book works as an inspiration to you. May it remind you that hope is always present, and the best is yet to come. Live your life fully, embrace happiness, embark on adventures, express yourself freely. Dance in the rain, get that tattoo – pursue whatever brings you joy. For when the time comes, remember, no one will live your life for you."

Author_susana_barrios

Let others follow you by scanning your QR code

♪ **TikTok**

@AUTHOR_SUSANA_BARRIOSS_

susana.brrs@gmail.com

www.ingramcontent.com/pod-product-compliance
Lightning Source LLC
Chambersburg PA
CBHW021235090426
42740CB00006B/548